D1715099

The History of the Reign of Peter the Cruel, King of Castile and Leon. By John Talbot Dillon, ... In two Volumes. ... of 2

THE HISTORY OF THE REIGN OF PETER THE CRUEL, KING OF CASTILE AND LEON.

By JOHN TALBOT DILLON, Esq.
B. S. R. E.
MEMBER OF THE ROYAL IRISH ACADEMY OF SCIENCES, AND HONORARY MEMBER OF THE LITERARY AND PHILOSOPHICAL SOCIETY OF MANCHESTER.

VOL. II.

It is one of the noblest functions of history to observe and to delineate men, at a juncture when their minds are most violently agitated, and all their powers and passions are called forth. ROBERTSON'S Hist. of America.

LONDON:
Printed for W. RICHARDSON, at the Royal-Exchange.
M, DCC, LXXXVIII.

THE HISTORY OF THE REIGN OF PETER THE CRUEL, KING OF CASTILE AND LEON.

CHAPTER THE FIRST.

Traſtamara enters Caſtile at the Head of an Army of Foreigners.—The City of Calahorra opens its Gates to him.—He is proclaimed King of Caſtile and Leon.—Marches from Burgos, and from thence to Toledo.—Peter retreats to Seville.

A. D. 1366.

HITHERTO we have ſeen the King of Caſtile at the head of his army, as a dread ſovereign ſtriking terror into a diſaffected nobility, and waging an impolitic war againſt the king of Aragon, ready to employ every ſtratagem to oppoſe the ſuperior power and inimical diſpoſition of a prince who ravaged his kingdom with fire and ſword. We at preſent behold the affairs of Caſtile under a new aſpect, and its monarch attacked in his deareſt rights, by one of his ſubjects, ſupported by France and Aragon, againſt whom the King of Caſtile had to combat in the field, in addition to the inſurmountable diſguſt of his people, alienated from his government by a powerful faction.

PETER was at Seville when he heard of this premeditated invaſion, and of the march of the diſbanded ſoldiers, which the French had permitted Traſtamara to take into his pay. Theſe conſiſted of French, Germans, and Flemings, whom the peace of Bretigny had rendered deſperate, and were ready to follow any leader that offered.

SOME Engliſh gentlemen were not aſhamed to take the command of theſe ruffians, who, under the name of *Malandrins*, or Companions, fought ſeveral battles with the French, and committed great devaſtations; inſomuch, that even a ſentence of excommunication iſſued by the Pope was not ſufficient to put a ſtop to their outrages. Their numbers

bers daily encreasing, so as to compose a body of forty thousand men, Charles of France rejoiced at the opportunity of getting rid of these mercenaries, who were ready to fight for any prince who offered them pay; by which they formed a standing army of hirelings, eager for plunder, unknown before this period in the annals of Europe.

To prevent the ill consequences apprehended from such an invasion, the Castilian monarch set out for Burgos, and assembled his forces, making every preparation his active genius suggested to crush such a daring attempt of a desperate enemy, who aimed at nothing less than to deprive him of his Crown: for, notwithstanding the unpopular light in which he was generally held, there were many lords still attached to the royal cause; who, jealous of the Gusmans, and their numerous kindred, were ready to oppose the designs of Trastamara (A).

When the King had taken the command of his army, he was met by the lord D'Albret, who came from Guyenne to offer his services; representing, that among the Companions who had engaged to ſerve under Traſtamara, there were many relations of his, and of the houſe of Armagnac, who were well affected to the King of Caſtile; and he propoſed to Peter to take them into his pay, or gain them over by donations, by which means he would prevail on them to return home. The avaricious monarch, however, was deaf to all propoſitions of this kind that interfered with his finances: on which D'Albret left him ſoon after, and returned home.

THIS army of Malandrines was led on by the celebrated Bertrand de Gueſclin, a warrior of great renown, and, according to Hume, the firſt conſummate general that ever appeared in Europe, though it was ſaid he could not read. Among the French who followed De Gueſclin, there were the young count de la Marche, of the houſe of Bourbon, who engaged in this conteſt with a view to revenge the death of his late couſin, Blanche, queen of Caſtile, the lord Anthony de Beaujeu, the lord D'Endreghan marſhal of France, and many other barons of note.

FROM the Engliſh army under the Prince of Wales, conceiving it at firſt to be a croiſade againſt the Moors of Granada, there joined Traſtamara, ſir Hugh de Calverley, ſir Euſtace d'Ambrecourt, ſir

Matthew

Matthew Gournay, ſir Walter Hewit, ſir John Devereux, and ſir John Neville.

These adventurers having aſſembled at Avignon under De Gueſclin, and extorted one hundred thouſand livres from the pope, for which a tax was laid on the clergy, they then, with the addition of his bleſſing, proceeded to Montpellier. In their paſſage through Carcaſſone, they were well received by the duke of Anjou, governor of Languedoc; and finally rendezvouſed at Barcelona, where they were joined by the reinforcements of Aragon.

From hence they boldly marched forward, and reached Alfaro in Caſtile, where the loyal governor Inigo Lopez de Oroſco held the caſtle againſt them in the name of Peter; which obliged them to alter their route and proceed to Calahorra, the governor of which, Ferrand Sanchez de Tovar, in conjunction with the biſhop, ſurrendered the city on capitulation to Henry of Traſtamara.

Such was the ſingular fate of the city of Calahorra, the antient Caligurris, to be the firſt to ſhake off their allegiance to their ſovereign; at which the women tore their hair, and the people in general lamented their misfortune, recollecting the boasted fidelity of their citizens since the days of the Romans; whose character was so great, that the emperor Augustus, sensible thereof, had formed from amongst them, a body of life-guards for the protection of his person; yet they were now the first to receive an usurper. (B.)

During all these transactions, Peter never ventured to move forward; so far from it, his warlike spirit forsook him, and he seemed intimidated at this host of strangers who invaded his kingdom. Trastamara took advantage of this panic, and shewed his determination either to reign in Castile, or lose his life in the contest.

The hour now approached to animate his followers, and crown all his hopes. The army looked up with fondness to their favourite Henry, and were so zealous in his favour, that on the twelfth of March a body of men assembled at Calahorra, ventured to proclaim Henry of Trastamara, *King of Castile and Leon*; his brother Don Tello displaying the royal standard at the head of his troops, and the soldiers shouting, "Castile for King Henry."

The

The day was ſpent in rejoicing: all the officers paid their court to the new king, who, though his realm only conſiſted of one inſignificant city, began his reign by eſtabliſhing his houſhold, and making liberal grants of lands in Caſtile which he was not poſſeſſed of, diſpoſing by his ſimple *fiat* of every thing that was aſked for; by which means he endeared himſelf to his needy adventurers, who concluded ſoon to poſſeſs all the caſtles in Spain, and to divide the whole kingdom amongſt them.

With theſe flattering ideas, the troops of Traſtamara took the field in great exultation, and attacked Bribieſca, which was taken by aſſault. This new acquiſition redoubled their joy, being now only eight leagues from Burgos; which city Peter reſolved to abandon, and fly from Traſtamara.

The King's horſe was ſaddled, and brought to the gate of his palace, when the Magiſtrates came, and preſſed him to remain with his faithful citizens of Burgos, who were ready to defend him with their lives and fortunes. All their intreaties, however, proved fruitleſs; Peter thanked them for their loyalty, and told them, it was neceſſary to return to Seville, to protect that city and his children from the evil deſigns of Traſtamara and his followers. The citizens replied, that his Grace was miſinformed; that Traſtamara and the Companies were certainly coming to Burgos, which his faithful citizens were ready to defend to the laſt extremity, if their ſovereign would ſtay with them.

The governor of the caſtle where the treaſury was kept, repeated the ſame; when, finding no entreaty could prevail, and that the King had not ſpirit to defend his own dominions, though his ſubjects were ready to lay down their lives in his defence, they requeſted to know what they were to do after his departure, if attacked by a ſuperior force. To this the King only ſaid, *I order you to do the beſt you can.*——"Since this is "your Grace's pleaſure, they replied, do you "free us from the oath of allegiance we have "taken to your perſon and government?——He anſwered, *Yes, yes*; and then ordered Tovar, the brother of the governor of Calahorra, to be put to death; after which ill-timed ſeverity, Peter fled from the city, attended by Don Martin Lopez de Cordova, and Inigo Lopez de Orofco, eſcorted by ſix hundred Mooriſh horſe, diſpatching expreſſes

expreſſes to all his governors in Aragon, to diſmantle the fortreſſes under their command, and join him with all ſpeed with the troops. So great was the King's panic, that he only halted at Lerma to dine, and then puſhed on for Gumiel de Yzam, twelve leagues from Burgos.

As for the people of Aragon, when the citizens of Calatayud ſaw themſelves freed from the Caſtilian yoke, they made ſolemn proceſſions of thankſgiving to the church of Our Lady *de la Pena* for their deliverance from the enemy: many in their retreat joined Traſtamara, while the bulk of the army continued ſtedfaſt in their allegiance, and followed the King. Among theſe latter were Don Garcia Alvarez de Toledo, maſter of the knights of St. James, who commanded at Logrono; Garcia de Padilla, governor of Agreda; Fernando de Toledo, brother to the maſter of St. James; and Boccanegra, admiral of Caſtile.

The infatuated Peter, however, ſtung with remorſe, ſeemed aſhamed of his conduct, and loſt all exertion; for when Orofco repreſented to him that there were many Engliſh knights whoſe valour and attachment to royalty was conſpicuous, who had made propoſals to defend him againſt any uſurper, he ſlighted their offers, and haſtened towards

towards Seville, not even ſtopping in the city of Toledo further than to appoint the maſter of St. James governor thereof, leaving ſix hundred horſe for his defence, and puſhing forward with the utmoſt precipitation; by which puſillanimous conduct he diſheartened his friends, and induced many to go over to Traſtamara, to whoſe proceedings at Calahorra we muſt now give a retroſpect.

The citizens of Burgos, ſeeing themſelves deſerted by their ſovereign, and expoſed to the hoſtile attacks of the other party, as well as freed from their oath of allegiance, ſent meſſengers to Traſtamara, inviting him to their city. This agreeable invitation was very acceptable to Henry, who immediately marched forward from Bribieſca, and was received in the city of Burgos with univerſal joy, the nobility in particular teſtifying their approbation, and evincing their readineſs to ſupport him. They conducted him to the royal monaſtery of *Las Huelgas* (C), and with the uſual ceremonies crowned him in the church, and proclaimed him King of Castile and Leon, all the lords preſent kiſſing his hand, and giving their ſanction to this important act.

The repreſentatives of the commons for many cities of the Cortes, came alſo to Burgos, and

and in the name of their conſtituents acknowledged the regal title of Henry of Traſtamara, who on his part granted every thing they aſked, and diſpenſed his favours with ſo liberal a hand, that none departed from his preſence diſſatisfied.

To De Gueſclin he gave the lordſhip of Molina and Soria, ordering him to aſſume the title of duke of Molina (D). To the count of Denia, of the royal line of Aragon, who followed him from that kingdom, he gave lands in Caſtile belonging to his wife, and conferred on him the title of marquis of Villena. To Don Tello de Caſtilla, his brother, he gave the lordſhip of Biſcay, with thoſe of Lara, Aguilar, and Caſtaneda, directing him to ſtile himſelf count of Biſcay (E). To his brother Don Sancho he gave the lordſhip of Alburquerque, with its dependencies, belonging to the deceaſed prime miniſter, John Alfonſo de Alburquerque, whoſe only ſon Don Gil was lately dead in Seville; and directed Don Sancho to ſtile himſelf count of Alburquerque; giving him further the lordſhip of Ledeſma, with many other lands. To ſir Hugh de Calverley he granted the lands of Carrion, with the title of count thereof (F). Many others were alſo rewarded according to their real or pretended ſervices. In a word,

word, there was no end to the largeſſes of Henry the Bountiful; which juſtifies the obſervation of a Britiſh hiſtorian, that "Conquerors, though uſually the bane of mankind, proved often in thoſe feudal times the moſt indulgent of ſovereigns."

Thus the bountiful and politic Henry, to ingratiate himſelf further with the people, renewed the feudatory titles of dukes, marquiſes, and counts, in Caſtile, which were at that time in diſuſe, except among the Infantes; more parcularly the title of duke. Even ſo great a lord as Don John Manuel, ſon of the infante Don Manuel, and grandſon of king Ferdinand III. proprietor of the lordſhip of Villena and many other fees, and the greateſt ſubject in the kingdom, could never obtain the ducal title from Alfonſo XI. (G.) So that we may eaſily conclude how acceptable this deviſe of the baſtard Henry muſt have proved to his followers, and the nobility who invited him into the kingdom.

Such were the effects of this ſudden proclamation of Henry, who in the courſe of twenty-five days ſaw himſelf maſter of great part of Caſtile, which voluntarily acknowledged him their ſovereign, the cities of Agreda, Soria, Laredo, and Logrono

Logrono excepted, who remained ſteady to Peter, as well as the kingdom of Galicia, where Fernan de Caſtro was governor; their example was followed by St. Sebaſtian's and Guetaria; and to the ſouthward, by the kingdom of Murcia, which to the laſt retained its fidelity; while in the northern parts, every day was diſtinguiſhed by new acquiſitions in favour of Henry.

Many lords of Caſtile and Leon came to his court at Burgos; amongſt others, that ungrateful favourite Diego Garcia de Padilla, who owed his fortune to Peter; but, having been coolly looked on, after the battle of Guadix, now deſerted his royal maſter, notwithſtanding all the favours that had been heaped on him, and his family: and ſo fatal are the conſequences of bad example, that he was followed by Inigo Lopez de Oroſco, Pero Gonzales de Mendoza, Garcilaſſo de la Vega, and others, who now revenged themſelves of the injuries they and their families had received.

Henry marched triumphantly forward to the city of Toledo, where great diſſenſions prevailed reſpecting the acknowledgment of his authority; however, the majority being in his favour, they obliged the brave Toledo (H), who had held out as long as he could, to open the gates to Henry, who made a public entry into the city amidst the acclamations of the citizens; and nothing was witnessed for fifteen days, but a constant scene of festivity and rejoicing, the people exclaiming incessantly, LONG LIVE HENRY, KING OF CASTILE, WHO FREED US FROM TYRANNY AND SLAVERY.

THE treasury was immediately seized, and out of it, the mercenary Companions were paid for their services, to keep them in temper. The Jews also advanced Henry a million of maravedis, towards defraying the charges of his government.

To give further weight to this authority, delegated by the people, the representatives in the Cortes for the cities of Avila, Segovia, Talavera, Cuenca, and Villareal, came to Toledo, and kissed the hand of their new sovereign, in token of their acquiescence to his authority; after which, the adventurous Henry made every disposition to protect and secure those rights, to which the Castilians had invited him. He therefore put himself at the head of his army, reinforced by many of his friends, and began his march towards Andalusia, in quest of his brother and sovereign King Peter.

CHAP.

CHAPTER THE SECOND.

Peter retires into Portugal, and from thence to Galicia, and embarks for Bayonne.—Goes from thence to Bourdeaux.—Is kindly received by the Prince of Wales, who raiſes an Army in favour of Peter, and marches into Caſtile.—The Baſtard Henry gets poſſeſſion of the City of Seville, and all the Kingdom of Andaluſia.—Duplicity of the King of Navarre.

THE fugitive Peter had no ſooner reached the city of Seville, than his firſt care was to look after, and ſecure his jewels. Terrified at the thoughts of being purſued by the baſtard Henry, who now jointly bore with him the title of KING OF CASTILE, he ordered Martin Yanez to convey his treaſures on board a ſwift-ſailing veſſel, and proceed with all diſpatch to Tavira in Portugal, and there wait for further inſtructions; while himſelf propoſed going by land to his uncle the king of Portugal, ſending forward his daughter Beatrix, who was betrothed to the Infante Don Pedro, heir to the king-

kingdom of Portugal, offering to ſettle on her the crown of Caſtile, and to give her beſides in money the fortune he had promiſed, with the jewels belonging to her mother, Maria de Padilla; all which were intruſted to Martinez de Truxillo, a confidential ſervant, who attended on the lady to Liſbon.

While Peter was concerting meaſures in this alarming ſituation, nothing but bad news daily haunted his palace. The firſt was the intelligence that Henry, having been proclaimed king of Caſtile by a great part of the nobility, was in full march towards Seville, with a numerous army: no anſwer from his uncle of Portugal; and to compleat his diſtreſs, news was brought that the city was in a ſtate of revolt, and the inhabitants advancing to plunder his palace!

On this, the affrighted monarch fled with all ſpeed from his favourite Alcazar in Seville (I), and retired towards Portugal, taking with him his other two daughters, Conſtance and Iſabel, attended by Martin Lopez de Cordova, maſter of Calatrava, with a few other gentlemen.

On

On the road he had the mortification to meet meſſengers from Portugal, ſtating that he could not be received in that kingdom, nor the Infante be permitted to marry his daughter, whom he had juſt overtaken on the road. On this Peter turned off towards Alburquerque, where they ſhut the gates againſt him. Here ſome of thoſe few who followed him, deſerted him, and took ſhelter in the caſtle of Alburquerque.

To heighten this diſappointment, he heard that the admiral Boccanegra had joined Henry, ſtopt his galley in the river of Seville, and ſeized the treaſure; on which the ill-fated prince, reduced almoſt to a ſtate of deſperation, diſpatched a perſon to the king of Portugal, ſupplicating a ſafe-conduct into Galicia, being fearful of the reſentment of the Infante Don Pedro of Portugal, who was nephew to Henry of Traſtamara, his mother being half-ſiſter to the lady Jane Manuel, the wife of Henry.

The king of Portugal ſent Don Alvaro Perez de Caſtro, and John Alfonſo Tello, count of Barcelos, with directions to eſcort Peter to Galicia; but when they had reached La Guardia, they pretended they could not proceed any farther, for

 fear

fear of the Infante, who had threatened them with his displeasure, if they went with King Peter; but on receiving six thousand doblas, two elegant poignards, and two costly girdles, richly ornamented, they were induced to go on, but left him at Lamego.

The King then went to Chavez, and reached Monterey in Galicia, in a most disconsolate plight. Here he staid three weeks, sending expresses to the king of Navarre, the Prince of Wales, and to the few friends he had left in Castile. Some advised him to go to Zamora, which declared for him, and whose citadel was commanded by sir John Gascoigne, a knight of St. John of Jerusalem. Astorga likewise retained its allegiance, as did Logrono and Soria in Castile; the faithful Soria, built on the remains of the antient Numantia, whose inhabitants in former days sustained a long and remarkable siege against the Romans.

The King received the disagreeable tidings, that Henry had taken possession of the city of Seville. He was advised to head his soldiers, and march into Galicia, and shew himself once more as a king to his subjects. Fernando de Castro was of this opinion; but the contrary prevailed, and it was agreed to go to the Groyne, and take

take ſhipping for Bayonne, to ſolicit ſuccours from the Prince of Wales.

In fine, the King, who, before his timid retreat from Burgos, had ever ſhewn the greateſt reſolution and valour, now exhibited the moſt daſtard and puſillanimous conduct, and was as perfectly deſerted by his friends, as a modern monarch had been at the cloſe of the laſt century; with this difference, that the laſt prince abdicated his crown to obtain aid from an abſolute monarch, who avowed to hold his kingdom only from God; while the cruel Peter, on leaving his dominions, flew for redreſs to the gallant Engliſh, famed for their love of liberty, the very ſons of thoſe who had ſo boldly ſtruggled to obtain Magna Charta, the pure fountain of their freedom.

Even this flight of the King could not be effected without traces of bloodſhed; for in paſſing through St. Jago, in his way to the Groyne, the archbiſhop of that city, who had dined with the King, being ſummoned to a council in the evening, was murdered at the gates of the city, as was the dean of the church, at the foot of the great altar; which ſhocked all ranks, for the archbiſhop was nephew to Garcia de Toledo, and had juſt joined the King with two hundred horſe, and lived in a caſtle belonging to his fee, near the city of St. Jago.

PETER after this made the beſt of his way for the Groyne, where he fitted out a galley to tranſport him to Bayonne, taking with him all the ſhipping he could meet on the coaſt. Leaving the command of Galicia and Leon to Fernando de Caſtro, he embarked for Bayonne, with a fleet of twenty two ſail, having with him his three daughters, and as much treaſure as he could collect, making about thirty thouſand gold piſtoles.

ON the news reaching the Prince of Wales, of his arrival, he ſent to him the lord of Poyanne, with ſeveral other gentlemen: meantime the King proceeded in a galley to Cape Breton, where he was met by the Prince of Wales, who conducted him to Bordeaux, and received him with great hoſpitality. Here he was waited on by Charles king of Navarre, when theſe great perſonages were entertained at a ſumptuous banquet; the Prince of Wales ſitting in the middle, the King of Caſtile on the right, and the king of Navarre on the left.

WITH

WITH this latter prince Peter entered into new engagements, to secure his passage into Castile, thro' the passes of Roncevalles. Nothing could be more liberal than Peter's offers; his golden promises were boundless, engaging to give to the king of Navarre for ever, all the land on the banks of the river, on both sides of Corunna; the town, castle, and appertenances of Salvatierra; with the town of St. John Pie du Port, and the marches thereabout, which had been violently taken from him. Moreover, he engaged to pay to the king of Navarre twenty thousand franks, to secure the passes of Roncevalles for his troops; and that they should be supplied with provisions. The King also entered into a bond to the Prince of Wales, for the sum of five hundred and fifty thousand florins of Florence, of good gold, for payment of his army.

PETER then went to Angouleme, and paid his compliments to the Princess of Wales, where he was again received with great splendour. The King presented to this lady many precious jewels, and to the Prince he further gave a rich table of curious workmanship, decorated in a most elegant manner with gold and precious stones; which table, some years after, in consideration of three hundred marks only, paſſed from the Prince to Doctor Thomas Arundel, biſhop of Ely, who left it by will to his ſucceſſors for ever; but, from ſome accident, it has long ſince diſappeared.

THE Prince of Wales not only promiſed to aſſiſt the King, but likewiſe aſſured him he would write to his father king Edward in his behalf, though many of his courtiers endeavoured to diſſuade him from it. The King then returned to Bayonne; but before his departure, to eternize his gratitude to the Engliſh nation, and teſtify his high regard for the Prince of Wales, he granted unto King Edward and the Prince his ſon, and to their heirs and ſucceſſors, kings and princes of England, for ever, "that when it ſhould pleaſe "any of them to be in perſon with the kings of "Caſtile, againſt any king of Granada, or other "enemy of the Chriſtian faith, they ſhould have "pre-eminence, and the chief place in the van, "above all other princes of Chriſtendom; and "though none of them ſhould be there in "perſon, yet there ſhould always be provided by "the kings of Caſtile, and their ſucceſſors, one "ſtandard of the arms of England, to be borne in the "ſame place for ever, for the honour of England,

"at

"at the proper coſt and charge of the King of "Caſtile." This inſtrument, ſigned by the King, bears date at Libourne, in the dioceſe of Bourdeaux, September 23d, 1366; and was afterwards ratified at Bayonne, in preſence of John de London, clerk of the dioceſe of Wincheſter, and apoſtolic notary, on the 11th of February, 1367.

THE King of Caſtile, further to gratify the Prince of Wales, agreed that he ſhould have the caſtles of Bermejo and Lequitio, with the lordſhip of Biſcay, and the caſtle of Urdiales, to hold, himſelf and his heirs, for ever, at his pleaſure, diſcharged from all appeal to any ſuperior lord, and as free as the kings of Caſtile had held the ſame heretofore; all which was confirmed under the great ſeal of Caſtile, both the original and duplicates of which remain in England to this day.

THESE matters being thus ſettled, the Prince of Wales, in order to ſupport the intereſt of King Peter, ſent heralds into Spain, enjoining all the Engliſh or Gaſcoigne knights who were with Henry the Baſtard, to repair to his ſtandard with all ſpeed; whereupon ſir Hugh de

Calverley, sir Eustace d'Ambricourt, sir Walter Hewit, sir John Devereux, sir John Neville, and others, took their leave of the Bastard, who dismissed them with courtesy; and many officers of the Companies followed them, who, not being in the secret, concluded a war was near at hand between England and France.

King Peter on his side was no sooner returned to Bayonne, than he dispatched Don Martin Lope de Cordova to England with the following instructions; by which we find that proposals of marriage with one of the daughters of England were part of this commission.

"What you, Don Martin Lope de Cordova, "shall say to the most illustrious and potent Edward king of England, our beloved cousin, shall "be as follows: You will relate the disturbances "and ferment which Don Henry has raised in our "dominions, striving to force us out of our kingdoms of Castile and Leon, which we hold by "legal inheritance, and not by tyranny, as Henry "alleges; taking great pains to insinuate most "treacherously to the holy father, and in France, "that we ought not to reign, because we govern "our kingdom with cruelty, and treat the lords "and

"and commons with injuſtice; whereas you will "repreſent that this is not the caſe, as is notorious. "We came lawfully to our eſtate, at the demiſe of "our honoured father king Alfonſo, when we "were minor, without experience; while our baſe-"brothers Henry and Frederic were more ad-"vanced in years, and ſhould have ſupported "our right, and given us good counſel; inſtead "of which, they endeavoured to dethrone us, and "conſpired with the nobility for that purpoſe in "the city of Medina Sidonia. But Providence "having preſerved us that time from their evil-"doings, they contrived other devices to leſſen us "in the opinion of our ſubjects; and becauſe we "would not conſent to every thing according to "their wiſhes, they treated us in the manner well-"known to you, in our city of Toro. With re-"ſpect to our having put Don Frederic to death, "he well deſerved it, for that, and other treaſons. "You will further repreſent, that Henry calls us "cruel and a tyrant, for having puniſhed thoſe "who diſobeyed us, and did great injury to our "faithful ſubjects; and you will add, what we "have verbally informed you, of the evil-do-"ings of thoſe whom we puniſhed. You will "further relate from us, every thing your own "prudence will ſuggeſt, to accompliſh what we

"deſire,

"desire, relative to the other requisitions you have "with you, under our hand, to promote the mar- "riages we have spoken to you about."

THE very idea of so open an attempt upon royalty in those feudal times, a right held so sacred and inviolable, would probably have been sufficient; but were now amply so, when thrown into the scale of political advantages, from a connection with Castile.

IT was therefore resolved in the council of Edward, that it was noble and honourable, as well as just and advantageous, to assist Peter, in his legal right. Accordingly king Edward gave leave to his son, John duke of Lancaster, to go to his brother the Prince of Wales, in support of the King of Castile, with four hundred chosen men at arms, and as many archers, followed by several hundred knights and English volunteers, who were desirous of displaying their gallantry and courage in Spain. This news gave the Prince much pleasure, as well as Peter: he made every preparation, and, exclusive of his own subjects in Aquitaine, engaged with much difficulty, the Companions from different parts of France, who fought their way through, plundering

plundering and pillaging the countries where they paſſed, and at laſt came ſafe, to the number of twelve thouſand men.

The King of Caſtile alſo made many levies, through the influence of the Prince of Wales, who, on his part, generouſly melted down two-thirds of his plate, and had it coined into money, which he diſtributed among the troops, and applied to his father for the ſum of one hundred thouſand franks, which was ſoon to be paid from France, as the remainder of king John's ranſom; which being granted, and the money paid in conſequence by the French, was ſent to the Prince, and given to the army in the ſame liberal manner.

Peter, further to ſecure the king of Navarre, and the paſſes through his country, agreed to cede to him the provinces of Guypuzcoa and Alava, with the town of Victoria; and ſuch other places as the king of Navarre alleged to have formerly belonged to him; who having more to fear from the Prince of Wales than from Henry, promiſed all that was aſked, as well as to ſerve in perſon in this expedition. King Peter, to attach the Prince ſtill further to his ſuit, promiſed

mised to sir John Chandos, his Privado, the town of Soria in Old Castile. It was also agreed upon, that the three daughters of the King, by Maria Padilla, should remain in Bayonne as hostages, along with the wives of the master of Alcantara, and of Matheo Fernandez, with the two sons of the latter.

Every thing being thus settled, the Prince of Wales and his new ally held themselves in readiness to begin their march towards Spain; but as the Princess was near her time, she expressed great uneasiness at the Prince's departure, and prevailed on him to remain at Bordeaux till her delivery; which happened the 6th of January following, on the feast of the Epiphany; when she was delivered of a prince, named Richard of Bordeaux, who afterwards succeeded to the throne of England, on the demise of his grandfather, and was the second of that name.

About this time, another splendid suitor, as a distressed king, implored the magnanimous support of our illustrious Edward. This was James the younger, titular king of Majorca, who, at that time, possessed not a foot of land in his nominal kingdom; his uncle Peter, king of Aragon, having, as was ſaid, murdered his father in priſon in Barcelona, and excluded him by force from that ſucceſſion; ſo that he had nothing left for his ſupport but the generoſity of Jane, queen of Jeruſalem, Sicily, and Naples; who, in conſideration of his youth, comely figure, and noble birth, had taken him for her third huſband, about four years before; and he now claimed the generous aſſiſtance of the Prince, to recover his kingdom.

THE Prince gave him a courteous and hoſpitable reception, with promiſe of ſupport on a future day. In the interval he followed the army, and determined to ſerve with King Peter, in his expedition to Caſtile.

BEFORE we proceed in our narrative relating to this memorable expedition, we muſt return to the proceedings of the Baſtard, after the retreat of Peter from Caſtile.

THE city of Seville no ſooner ſaw themſelves freed from the vexations and reſentment of their monarch, than they made every preparation to welcome his opponent. So great was the concourſe, of all ranks, to behold the entrance of Henry into that

that city, that though he appeared early in the day before their walls, it was a late hour in the evening before Henry and his attendants could reach the alcazar, or palace, where he was received with tumultuous joy by the magiſtrates and citizens.

THE city of Cordova followed their example, and ſubmitted to Henry, as did the whole province of Andaluſia.

THE Mooriſh king of Granada haſtened likewiſe to renew treaties of amity and alliance with Henry, as the ſovereign of Caſtile; verifying the noted Spaniſh proverb, which had taken its riſe under Alfonſo X. "That the departed and the ab-" "ſent are bereft of friends." (H.)—Of this Peter ſtood a recent proof. The admiral of Caſtile, Boccanegra, on whom he had accumulated many favours, now, to ingratiate himſelf with Henry, alſo betrayed his truſt, in the manner related; and made Yanez, the King's treaſurer, a priſoner. Even Yanez himſelf, dreading the reſentment of Peter, alſo deſerted his maſter, and ſided with Henry.

THERE

There were found on board this galley thirty-ſix quintals of gold, and a great number of jewels and precious ſtones, with which the Baſtard paid his foreign troops, and ſatisfied the moſt preſſing applications. In recompence of the treachery of Boccanegra, he had a grant from Henry of the town of Otiel, with its juriſdiction, which was ſettled for ever on his family. All ranks were ſatisfied by the bountiful Henry; and the citizens of Seville obtained every thing they aſked for from their new ſovereign, eager to engage the good will and affections of the people.

Here he received news of the ſucceſsful negotiations of Peter in Bourdeaux; it was therefore high time to take the field, and reduce by arms, thoſe provinces which adhered to their ſovereign, and refuſed to acknowledge the authority of Henry.

For this purpoſe, he ſet out for Galicia to attack Fernando de Caſtro, who commanded there for King Peter. Henry beſieged him in the town of Lugo; but the loyal and faithful Gallicians made ſo vigorous a defence, that Henry was obliged to retreat, and retire to Burgos. Here he convened the Cortes, and conſulted them on the beſt meaſures to be taken for the ſafety of the kingdom;

kingdom; aſſuring them that he was ready to lay down his life in defence of their liberties.

The Cortes unanimouſly agreed to ſupport Henry with their lives and fortunes, and granted new ſupplies for the exigencies of government.—Here ambaſſadors came from the king of Aragon, reminding Henry of his former engagements and treaties, claiming the cities and territories he had promiſed, as well as the ſums expended, in ſetting him on the throne of Caſtile. To theſe unwelcome gueſts Henry gave the beſt anſwer he could, repreſenting his critical ſituation at that moment; and with evaſive profeſſions and fair promiſes diſmiſſed them.

Henry then attached himſelf to the king of Navarre, whoſe friendly aid he courted with the utmoſt aſſiduity. To ſecure the intereſt of that crafty ſovereign, he held a conference with him, attended by De Gueſclin, in the town of Santa Cruz de Campeza, and gave him 6000 doblas to open the paſſes of Roncevalles, and prevent King Peter from penetrating into Caſtile. The town of Logrono, which had already been offered by Peter, was again promiſed by Henry; ſo that the wily king of Navarre, between both, thought himſelf

ſure

ſure of his mark, as well as to make a good bargain for himſelf between two competitors, who were outbidding each other, and ſetting up the whole kingdom to auction.

Notwithstanding therefore his prior engagements, he promiſed every thing to Henry; and then, to avoid fulfilling his word to either, he contrived a ſcheme, with ſir Oliver Manny, a relation of De Gueſclin's, who held for him the town of Borja in Aragon, ceded in the late war, by which he might dupe both the candidates for his favour.

It was concerted amongſt them, that on a future day the king of Navarre ſhould repair to the city of Tudela, only four leagues from Borja, under pretence of a hunting-party, when Manny was ſuddenly to appear and take the king priſoner, which would prevent his appearance in the field, in behalf of King Peter, according to promiſe. With this duplicity the king of Navarre thought to deceive both parties, forward his own views, and ſcreen himſelf from the reſentment of either.

CHAPTER THE THIRD.

King Peter and the Prince of Wales march into Castile.—Henry advances with a Design of giving them Battle.—Sends a Herald to the Prince of Wales, and encamps near Nagera.—The King of Castile and the Prince of Wales obtain a Victory over Henry at Nagera.—Henry flies into Aragon.——Peter recovers his Kingdom by the Aid of the English.

A. D. 1367.

WE now resume the operations of King Peter, and his march into Caſtile, ſupported by an Engliſh army, led on by the Prince of Wales.

ON the Sunday following the delivery of the Princeſs of Wales, the magnanimous Prince, eager to ſupport his Spaniſh ally, ſet out from Bordeaux, and repaired to the head-quarters of the army, at Dax in Gaſcony, leaving Gaſton earl of Foix, with the lord James Audley, in the government of Aquitaine during his abſence.

THE

THE Prince was joined at Dax by Peter and the duke of Lancaſter, and meaſures were concerted for their immediate progreſs towards Caſtile. During their ſtay at Dax, rumours had ſpread that the king of Navarre had betrayed them, treated with the Baſtard, and offered him a paſſage through his country. The report had gained ſuch credit, that ſir Hugh de Calverley had marched forward, and taken poſſeſſion of Puente de la Reyna, and the city of Miranda, belonging to the king of Navarre. This brought on an explanation; and at an interview between the King of Caſtile, the king of Navarre, the Prince of Wales, and ſir John Chandos, all matters were amicably adjuſted. The king of Navarre found himſelf neceſſitated to make good his engagements, and grant a free paſſage through his kingdom, for which Peter paid him the twenty thouſand franks agreed on; after which the Caſtilian monarch and the Prince returned to Dax, and were further joined by the lord Oliver Cliſſon from Brittany, the lord John de Grailly, Captal of Buſche, and the Count D'Albret.

THIS grand army was now ſet in motion to reſtore a valiant and lawful ſovereign to his dominion, and approached, through a rugged country, those dangerous paſſages under the Pyrenean mountains, which lie between St. John de Pied de Port and the city of Pampelona, rendered ſtill more difficult at that inclement ſeaſon, by wind, hail, and ſnow, which fell in great quantities, it being about the end of February when this painful expedition was effected. But the courage of the Engliſh ſoldiers was ſuperior to all difficulties, and they happily ſurmounted every obſtacle.

The van of the army was led on by John of Gaunt, duke of Lancaſter, fourth ſon of king Edward, a prince of great ſtrength and courage, then in the flower of youth, being in the twenty-ſeventh year of his age, and honorably emulous of the glory of the Prince his brother. Under him followed the lord John Chandos, high-conſtable of Aquitaine. In the centre were the two marſhals of Aquitaine, ſir Guiſcard D'Angouleme, and ſir Stephen Coſſington, with the great banner of St. George. With the duke of Lancaſter were alſo ſir William Beauchamp, lord of Abergavenny, fourth ſon to the earl of Warwick, the lord Ralph Neville, with his eldeſt ſon ſir John Neville, ſir William Clayton, ſir John Tyrrel, ſir Hugh Haſtings,

Haſtings, ſir Robert Cheney, ſir William Boteler of Overſley in Warwickſhire, ſir Robert Willoughby, and others, forming a body of ten thouſand horſe. Theſe paſſed on the Monday.

On Tueſday came the Prince of Wales, followed by King Peter and the king of Navarre. In this diviſion were the lord Thomas Felton, and the lord William his brother, the lord Euſtace D'Ambrecourt, ſir Nele Loring Knight of the Garter the Prince's Grand Chamberlain, ſir Thomas Banniſter, and many other lords, with all the Poitevins, to the number of one thouſand men at arms, and ten thouſand horſe. Having paſſed with great difficulty on account of the bitterneſs of the weather, they encamped in the plains about Pampelona, to which city the king of Navarre invited and entertained the King of Caſtile and the Prince of Wales.

On the Wedneſday, the rear of the army paſſed alſo with the titular king of Majorca, the Count D'Armagnac, and his nephew the Count D'Albret, the Captal of Buſche, ſir Thomas Winſtanley and other lords, with the Companions, forming likewiſe another body of ten thouſand horſe.

HAVING all safely passed the Pyrenean mountains, they extended themselves in the plains of Navarre, the Companions ravaging the country in their usual manner, and devouring every thing like locusts, to the great displeasure of the king of Navarre; but there was now no remedy.

WHEN Henry heard that Peter, in conjunction with the Prince of Wales, had passed the straits of Roncesvalles, at the head of a formidable army of English, as well as Castilians, and the reinforcements from Brittany, there being a profound peace at that time between England and France, he collected all the forces he could; and being well beloved by the people, great numbers flocked to his standard; so that he soon assembled a considerable army, and fixed his head-quarters at St. Domingo de la Calzada, in Old Castile.

THE fame of the Prince of Wales's disciplined troops was well known in France, and messengers were sent to Henry, to caution him against giving battle; advising him rather to secure an advantageous position, till the enemy had consumed their provisions; when so considerable an army would be obliged to disperse of itself, and be fallen upon to

the

the greateſt advantage. But this good counſel ill ſuited the ardour of Henry. He made every diſpoſition for battle, though not yet joined by De Gueſclin; repreſenting to his followers, that if the enemy thought he was fearful to attack them, their own friends in Caſtile would be abaſhed, dreading the ſevere temper of Peter, and would return to their allegiance. Since therefore ſo many gallant gentlemen had ventured their lives in his ſupport, it ſhould not be ſaid that he was backward, as he was reſolved to give them the example, truſting to Providence and the valour of his countrymen for victory.

For theſe reaſons he determined to advance towards the enemy; and the better to diſplay his valour, and how worthy he was of that ſtation to which his countrymen had raiſed him, he ſaid aloud to the Caſtilian lords who ſurrounded him, "This Prince of Wales is a valiant knight; "and that he may know this realm is mine, "and that I am ready and willing to fight him "in ſupport of the right which I have thereto, "I will let him know ſome part of my intent." Then he cauſed his ſecretary to write to the Prince of Wales as follows:

"HENRY, by the grace of God, King of Castile "and Leon, of Galicia, Murcia, Jaen, Algarbe, "Algeziras, and Gibraltar, Lord of Biscay, and "Molina. To the right puissant and most honour-"able lord, Edward Prince of Wales and Aqui-"taine, duke of Cornwall, earl of Chester, greet-"ing: Whereas it is given us to understand, that "you and your men have passed the Pyrenees, "and are marching towards us, having entered "into strict alliance with our enemy, and intend "to wage war against us; we greatly marvel "thereat, since to our knowledge we never offend-"ed you, or ever had the least intent so to do: "Wherefore then are you come against us, with "such mighty force, to deprive us of that small "inheritance which Providence hath allotted us? "You have, we acknowledge, the good fortune "to be successful in arms above any prince now "living, and you magnify yourself in your puis-"sance! But since we know for certain, that you "intend to give us battle, we also hereby give "you to understand as certainly, that whenever "you advance in Castile, so surely you shall find "us in front, ready to defend and hold this our "seignory. Dated at St. Domingo de la Cal-"zada."

THIS

This letter was delivered to the Prince of Wales at Pampelona, who, when he read it, ſaid with his uſual ſpirit, "I well perceive the baſtard "Henry is a valiant knight, and ſheweth good "courage thus to write to us."—After a ſhort debate it was determined to detain the herald, and not give him any anſwer for the preſent: however, the Prince perceiving the reſolution of Henry, made every preparation for battle.

When the unexpected news was brought to the camp, that the king of Navarre (who was reſolved not to proceed any farther) had been taken priſoner by ſir Oliver Manny, in the manner related, the queen of Navarre pretended to be greatly diſtreſſed, and applied to the Prince, who ſent her home; after which, with the aſſiſtance of the guides of the king of Navarre, he puſhed forward, and reached Salvatierra in the province of Alava, then in the intereſt of Henry. However, on the approach of Peter, they preſented him with the keys, and made their ſubmiſſion, begging grace and pardon; which Peter granted, at the interceſſion of the Prince, though he wanted at firſt to put them all to the ſword, in terror to the reſt.

While

While the Prince was on his march to Salvatierra, ſir Thomas Felton and his company had taken poſt at Navaret, near Henry's camp, and brought word that Henry had moved from St. Domingo de la Calzada, and advanced to St. Miguel; on which the Prince of Wales eagerly went in queſt of the enemy, and advanced with all ſpeed as far as Victoria, where he was joined by ſir Thomas Felton, and got intelligence that Henry was in their neighbourhood, and made a reſolute ſtand.

Perceiving therefore the courage of the enemy, he loſt no time in marching towards them; and having drawn out the army, the Prince conferred the honour of knighthood, at the head of the army, on Peter King of Caſtile, and on the lord Thomas Holland, ſon to his princeſs by her former huſband, then about ſeventeen years of age; a gallant youth, eager to ſignalize himſelf in the field. The ſame honour was conferred on many Engliſh eſquires, as well by the duke of Lancaſter, as by the king of Majorca, who alſo made ſeveral knights, as did the lord John Chandos; ſo that there was no leſs than three hundred new knights made on that occaſion.

The

THE Engliſh army ſoon became in want of proviſions, and bread was ſo ſcarce, that a loaf ſold for a florin. Beſides, the troops ſuffered much from the inclemency of the weather, independent of the barrenneſs of the country. The Prince therefore hearing that Henry had broke up his camp at St. Miguel, and advanced to Nagera, where he halted, determined to draw towards him, and give battle to the Baſtard, and drive him out of the realm.

FINDING the entrance difficult on the ſide of Caſtile, he traverſed Navarre till he came to the town of Viana near the river Ebro; and after refreſhing the army for two days, he went forward to Logrono, and paſſed the Ebro over the bridge in that city; then entered Caſtile, where he found himſelf in a more plentiful country, with hopes ſoon to come up with the main army of Henry.

EVEN before he left his camp near Victoria, ſir Thomas Felton had moved forward, and fallen in with ſome of their advanced poſts; and finally was ſurrounded on a hill, and overpowered by numbers, when ſir Thomas and his brother, with many other gallant Engliſhmen, were unfor-

unfortunately killed at a place called Ariniz, about a league from Victoria; which hill is to this day called *Ingles-mond*, "the mount of the English."

The Prince of Wales now expecting every moment to engage the enemy, thought proper to dismiss the Spanish herald, and by him he sent to Henry the following answer to the letter he had received from him.

"Edward, by the grace of God, Prince of "Wales and Aquitaine, duke of Cornwall, and "earl of Chester. To the right honourable and "renowned Henry count of Trastamara, at present stiling himself king of Castile, greeting: "Whereas you have sent unto us your letters by "your herald, wherein are contained divers passages, intimating that you would gladly know "why we support the cause of our friend and ally, your enemy, our beloved cousin, Don Peter, "King of Castile, and by what title we make war "upon you, and enter with our army into Castile; to which we give you this answer. "Know, for a truth, that it is to sustain right "and justice, and to uphold reason and equity, as "it appertaineth to all kings and princes to do; "and

" and alfo to cultivate and cherifh the ftrict al-" liances which the king of England, our deareft" father, and King Don Peter have long time" fince held together. However, becaufe you" are a renowned and right valiant knight, we" are willing, as far as lays in us, to reconcile" you and King Don Peter together; and we fhall" fo perfuade our coufin Don Peter, that he fhall" yield unto you a confiderable portion of his" realm of Caftile: but as for the crown and" regal inheritance, That you muft renounce for" ever; in which cafe, Sire, you may take coun-" fel, and be advifed. As to our entrance into" the kingdom of Caftile, we will enter, and pro-" ceed forward, according as it may beft fuit our" own will and pleafure. Dated at Logrono the" 30th of March, 1367.

THIS bufinefs being fettled, the Prince began his march from Logrono on the 2d of April. Henry no fooner received this letter, and heard of his approach with King Peter, than he determined to move towards him. For this purpofe he drew near to the town of Nagera, and chofe a favourable fituation to pitch his camp, having the little river Nagerillo between him and the road which Peter was to pafs, before he could reach the

the city of Burgos. Not content with this diſpoſition, his anxious mind urged him to puſh forward. He boldly reſolved to croſs the river, and drew up his army on a plain, determined to diſpute the paſſage with the enemy; a meaſure which was not much approved of by his generals, as he relinquiſhed a very advantageous poſt, for one much leſs ſo: but the enterpriſing Henry declared he was reſolved to meet the enemy in the field, and conquer or periſh. De Gueſclin had lately joined him with four thouſand men from France; and his troops were in ſuch high ſpirits, that Henry, fluſhed with the flattering hopes of ſoon completing his conqueſt of Caſtile, panted eagerly for battle.

The army of the Prince of Wales now appeared in ſight, advancing briſkly, and in fine order, equally deſirous to bring on a general engagement, the Engliſh diſplaying the banner of St. George, and Henry that of Caſtile.—The antient chronicles are ſo prolix and minute in the deſcription of battles and names of combatants, that it would afford little pleaſure at this time of day, when the ſyſtem of war is ſo different, to detain the reader with the various arrangements of thoſe feudal troops, which our own hiſtorians have fully

fully defcribed. Suffice it to fay, that the van of the Englifh, commanded by John of Gaunt, duke of Lancafter, with fir John Chandos, attacked the divifion of the enemy commanded by Don Sancho, brother to the baftard Henry, and by De Guefclin; who, being ill fupported on the left wing, were foon drove back by the right wing of King Peter's divifion, commanded by the Count D'Armagnac and the Count D'Albret.

THE battle now became hot and general on both fides. Henry's army difplayed great courage, and were in excellent order for combat, being armed after the manner of France, which hitherto had not been introduced into Spain. The Spaniards alfo had flings; an ancient cuftom, which they ftill retained from the Romans; and with which they whirled ftones of a large fize, that galled the Englifh exceedingly: however, the Englifh archers were no lefs dexterous with their bows, and made great havock among their opponents.

HENRY rode with great ardour through the ranks, animating his men, faying to them, "My valiant friends, I am your king! You "have made me fo, and fworn to fupport me. Be "mindful

"mindful of your oath, and ſhew yourſelves "ſteady, for certainly I will not flinch one foot, "but ſtand by you to the laſt."—Again, when he found them giving way, he added with great animation, "Where is the courage of thoſe no- "ble Spaniards, who, under my father Alfonſo, "ſo wonderfully vanquiſhed the Moors? Do not "diſgrace yourſelves this day, by turning your "backs: a little more perſeverance will crown "your brows with victory."

King Peter was not leſs in earneſt, courageouſly ſaying to his ſubjects, "My brave countrymen, I "place all my hopes in your loyalty. Stand firm to "defend your king, to whom you have ſworn alle- "giance." Thus in the heat of the battle Peter was ſeen at the head of his men, much agitated with the violent reſiſtance he met with, wiſhing to meet the Baſtard, and exclaiming, "Where is this "ſon of a whore who calls himſelf king of Caſ- "tile? Let him face me if he dares."

After a long and dubious conflict, fortune at laſt declared in favour of the victorious Prince of Wales; for nothing could withſtand the valour and courage of the Engliſh, under the banners of their invincible leader. The Baſtard's army now gave way on all ſides, and fled with the utmoſt

preci-

precipitation, though their commander had done every thing to be expected from a courageous and consummate general; but all was in vain: the route was general, and Peter pressed them closely with infinite slaughter, following them into the town of Nagera, which they plundered. Here Henry lost all his equipage and treasure, many were drowned in the river, and the victory complete on the side of the English, who now hailed King Peter as the victorious sovereign of Castile and Leon.

The number of prisoners was also great; the principal of which were Don Sancho de Castilla, base brother to Peter, with that gallant soldier De Guesclin; also the Marshal d'Audenheim; the Begue de Vilaine; the Count of Denia, of the royal line of Aragon; Philip de Castro, brother-in-law to Henry (K); Pero Lope de Ayala the historian, and many other lords. Ayala being a poet, as well as an historian and a soldier, has recorded in verse the melancholy tale of his captivity. Inigo Lope de Orosco, whose desertion of his master we have related before, was killed by King Peter on the field of battle, for his treachery, after being taken prisoner by a Gascon knight. This signal victory was obtained on Saturday the third of April. The number of prisoners of rank was about two thousand, whereof about two hundred were French, and not a few Scotch.

The Prince of Wales enquired eagerly after Henry. Two knights with two heralds were sent to see if he could be found any where on the field, but all was in vain; and no tidings could be had, which made the Prince say, that "if the Bastard "was not killed or taken, the business was not "half completed."

The next day, Sunday, was spent in thanksgiving on the field of battle. King Peter requested permission of the Prince of Wales to put all his prisoners to death; which he would have done, if the generous Prince had not interposed; representing in very strong terms, that if he did not relax in the severity of his temper, and shew more lenity, all the power of England would be of little service. Peter urged on his side, that if he set all his enemies at liberty, they would raise new disturbances in his kingdom, and the contest as well as bloodshed would be endless. These differences of opinion caused much coolness between the King and the Prince, who consented that those should suffer against whom sentences had already

passed

paffed for rebellion in Peter's courts; in confe-quence of which Sanchez Mofcofo, Grand Com-mandeur of St. James, and Garci Jofre, fon of the Admiral, were put to death; as well as Gomez Carillo de Quintana, at whofe rebellious conduct Peter was fo incenfed, that he would accept of no ranfom for his life, and caufed his head to be ftruck off before his tent. However, at the Prince's requeft, he pardoned all the others, and was reconciled to his bafe-brother Don Sancho, and the other lords, his prifoners, on condition of their fwearing allegiance to him, and acknow-ledging him ever after, the only lawful King of Caftile and Leon.

THERE was now nothing but rejoicing in Peter's camp, and preparations were made to march towards Burgos, and get poffeffion of that important city. Meantime the King fent intelli-gence to all his friends, of his conqueft, and of his being once more, by the aid of the Englifh, in full poffeffion of his kingdom.

WHEN the news reached England, it was received with infinite joy. Notwithftanding the prejudices that might have been raifed againft Pe-ter by his enemies, the citizens of London particularly diſtinguiſhed themſelves on this occaſion; the lord-mayor and aldermen celebrated the memory of this battle, and Peter's ſucceſs, with triumphal arches, and all the pomp and parade in uſe in thoſe times for the victories of their own kings over their enemies.

CHAP.

CHAPTER THE FOURTH.

The King of Castile returns to the City of Burgos.—He is received with great Acclamations, and acknowledged again by his Subjects as their Sovereign.—The Prince of Wales enters into Negotiations for the Payment of the English Troops.—King Peter solemnly swears in the Cathedral of Burgos to pay all the Arrears due, then departs for Andalusia.—The Prince of Wales goes to the City of Valladolid.

IF History is not only a narrative of the actions of men, but further a faithful mirror of the human heart, we must expect to find the feelings and passions of the mind universally the same, though tinctured with various shades, in proportion to the more or less state of refinement or cultivation in civil society. Under every aspect, it will afford us important instruction, when we view the concomitant circumstances, and fully weigh the opinions and prejudices of the times, in order to form a solid and impartial judgment, and decide upon the equal poize of justice, between the parties before us.

In the dark age we are ſpeaking of, the tranſactions in Caſtile were not very different in the aggregate, from thoſe in England. The blood of the nobles in both countries was ſpilt copiouſly, civil rights were little underſtood in Europe, and the laws were inaccurate. An Engliſh baron varied little from a *Rico-ome* of Caſtile, whether he brandiſhed the lance, or hunted the beaſt of the foreſt; murders were not ſo heinouſly conſidered as at preſent; and many were committed, without conveying the idea of cruelty on the perpetrator.

That Peter's conduct might have been of this ſtamp, there is little room to doubt; but his provocations were great, and the accounts handed down are conveyed by his enemies, ſtrongly intereſted to blacken his fame, give colour to their own acquiſitions, and deprive him of his crown. That cruelty was a vice of which the greateſt characters of that age cannot be wholly acquitted, is evident from our own hiſtorians; witneſs the carnage, conflagrations, and ruin that attended the reign of our illuſtrious Edward and his ſon the Black Prince, notwithſtanding that blaze of glory by which their memories are ſurrounded; ſo that, inſtead of being the friends of mankind, we ſhall

more

more frequently find them the deſtroyers of the human race. Even the example of clemency given by the Prince of Wales after the defeat at Nagera, had not taken a deep root in his mind; for a few years after, when the Prince got poſſeſſion of Limoges, he maſſacred the French garriſon, with three thouſand inhabitants. Yet the crime of theſe citizens was ſimilar to the opponents of Peter, though they were unfortunately put to death by the ſame hand that interfered for the priſoners at Nagera. Peter pardoned, and was called THE CRUEL: Edward maſſacred, and was ſtyled THE MAGNANIMOUS; and Guyenne was loſt to England on the ſame principles as Caſtile to King Peter.

BUT we muſt now trace the ſequel of this melancholy ſtory, and view Peter reinſtated on his throne by his illuſtrious ally Edward III. king of England, and his invincible ſon. We have ſeen in what a puſillanimous manner the King of Caſtile deſerted his ſubjects at Burgos, and freed them from their allegiance. At preſent we view him recovered from his panic, after diſplaying the moſt heroic valour at the battle of Nagera, returning with a triumphant army to face thoſe very citizens, whom before he had so shamefully abandoned.

On the King's approach to Burgos, the citizens, having learned the defeat of the Bastard, were all submission to the conqueror. The principal lords and magistrates came out to welcome the King to his good city of Burgos, and presented him with the keys, in token of their submission; acknowledging him as their sovereign Lord and King, and conducting him to his palace with every demonstration of respect.

To evince that the passions of mankind have ever been the same, we have seen a similar scene in this country, in the person of the monarch already mentioned, who was observed to fly with pusillanimity from his capital, and a few days after make his entry into the same metropolis, amidst the shouts and acclamations of his subjects. Thus it happened with Peter; he was now once more publickly acknowledged the only true and lawful King of Castile, in Burgos, its capital.

The King's first care was to dispatch expresses to all his subjects, and particularly to his faithful kingdom of Murcia, to whom he addressed the following

following mandate: "Don Peter, by the grace "of God, King of Caſtile and Leon, &c. To "the worthy magiſtrates and council of the city "of Murcia, and to the officers holding juriſdic- "tion in our kingdom of Murcia, greeting. "Know ye, that on Saturday the 3d of April we "arrived near the town of Nagera, the Prince of "Wales and myſelf, with the king of Majorca, "the duke of Lancaſter, the count D'Armagnac, "and the other puiſſant lords and barons who "came to our aſſiſtance, when we gave battle to "that traitor the count, with his treacherous "aſſociates, who joined him in rebellion againſt "us; whom, thanks to the Almighty, who would "not permit might to overcome right, we van- "quiſhed. As for that traitor Henry, we do not "know whether he be taken, or be dead; though "we preſume one or the other has happened, as "moſt of the lords who were with him were ſlain, "the number of which is infinite. We there- "fore ſend ye this news, perſuaded it will re- "joice ye; whom we command, without wait- "ing further orders, to preſerve the kingdom of "Murcia in our name, and allegiance, ſeizing "all thoſe who take the part of that traitor, the "count, and proceeding againſt them in ſuch "manner as is fitting to our legal authority, in "ſupport

"support of our dominion. And thus may God "preserve ye in his holy keeping! Given at "Burgos, &c."

THE King's court was now fully eftablifhed at Burgos as heretofore, where he was immediately followed by the Prince of Wales and the other Englifh officers of rank, marching forward with the army, at the head of their different divifions. The royal and magnificent monaftery of *Las Huelgas*, in the fuburbs of Burgos, was affigned for the reception of the Prince of Wales; the duke of Lancafter was lodged in the convent of St. Paul, in the city; and the army was cantoned in the neighbouring villages. Every honour was fhewn by Peter to his illuftrious ally and protector, and nothing but feftivity and joy were feen in Burgos for feveral days fucceffively.

THE reprefentatives of Aftorga, Toledo, Leon, Galicia, Afturias, Bifcay, Cordova, and, in a manner, all his eftates fent addreffes to the King, full of profeffions of loyalty, as their true and lawful fovereign; fo that if any weight were to be given to public profeffions and addreffes, Peter might now think himfelf perfectly reftored to his right. But, alas! addreffes are only empty words, and too

too well known to be of little import, as Peter ſoon fatally experienced.

The Prince of Wales, ſuppoſing he had now perfectly reſtored his good couſin of Caſtile to his kingdom, thought proper, after a few days repoſe, to enter upon the buſineſs of his expedition, purſuant to the original agreements entered into at their departure from Bordeaux. He particularly ſtated, that he could not have led ſo gallant an army into Spain without incurring a conſiderable expence, part of which had already been advanced by the King at Bayonne; but there ſtill were conſiderable arrears due, for large ſums advanced to many lords, according to the ſtipulations agreed on; which matters the Prince beſought his Grace to take into conſideration, as he was now in poſſeſſion of his kingdom; reminding him, likewiſe, of his promiſes to grant him large eſtates in his realm of Caſtile, as well in caſtles as in lands, for which he again thanked him; though he had before declined any intereſted views, and was ready to ſerve his Grace, in virtue of the ties and alliances between them, and the ſtrict charge given him by his honoured ſire, the king of England, to aſſiſt him with all his might: That ſince the offers of the King of Caſtile

Caſtile had been made out of his Grace's free will and pleaſure, he nevertheleſs declined holding any eſtates in Caſtile, but rather deſired to be confirmed in the grant of the lordſhip of Biſcay, according to the tenor of the vouchers under his Grace's hand, which he was ready to produce.

THE Prince then ſtated the general expences of the army, which was now of no further uſe; and expreſſed his deſire to return home, when theſe matters were adjuſted; as well to free the King from ſuch a heavy charge, as to attend to his own concerns in Guyenne, where the French factions, during his abſence, had begun to raiſe cabals, which made his preſence eſſentially neceſſary.

PETER laid all theſe points before his privy council, who in his name gave for anſwer to the Prince of Wales, "that with reſpect to the agree-"ment at Bayonne, the Prince knew the King "had advanced large ſums, as well in gold and "ſilver ſpecie, as in jewels and precious ſtones, "by all which he had been a great loſer; for not "only the jewels, but even the coin had been re-"ceived at a rate far beneath their value; which "his Treaſurer had frequently repreſented at the "time, but to no effect. It was therefore recom-

"mended

" mended that thofe accounts might be audited; " and if any deficiencies were difcovered, the " King was ready to make them good; though " he believed, when the fums were ftated with " accuracy, that nothing would be found due " from him to the Englifh army.

" THAT with refpect to the lordfhip of Bifcay, " and town of Caftro de Urdiales, it was all true, " and the King was ready to confirm the fame, " and cede them to the Prince immediately.

" THAT for the Prince's defire to return home, " and eafe him of the burthen of foreign troops, " he thanked him kindly, and left him to ufe his " pleafure: but if he would leave him fome men " at arms, and a thoufand lances, to be paid for " in Caftile, till matters were quieted, he fhould " be very thankful."

WHEN the Prince heard this anfwer he replied, " that refpecting the troops, his Grace had " given fuch anfwer as fuited his pleafure; but " to the point in queftion, it was no fault of his, " as the King's Treafurer did juft as he pleafed: " That the officers had often complained of the " great lofs fuftained in receiving jewels and " pearls,

" pearls, which they were obliged to ſell at a great " loſs, to purchaſe horſes and furniture.

" Besides, the King muſt have known, that ſo " many great lords and their vaſſals did not come " at the charge of the king of England, but from " their attachment to that ſovereign and to him- " ſelf, added to thoſe engagements in which " the Prince in his own name ſtood bound to " them; which he waved enlarging upon, hoping " the King of Caſtile would reward them nobly, " and becoming the dignity of his Crown.

" For the lordſhip of Biſcay, he repeated his " thanks, and deſired immediate orders might be " given accordingly. As for the lances requeſted, " he was willing they ſhould remain; but for the " men at arms, he could ſay nothing at preſent, " as he wiſhed to know how they were to be paid."

On the ſubject of all theſe articles there was much debate, which produced every day more coolneſs on both ſides; the Prince thinking himſelf very ungenerouſly and unjuſtly treated; the King not willing, or perhaps not able at that critical juncture to fulfil his engagements any further, ſupported only by the terror of foreign troops,

troops, which would no ſooner leave him, than his authority would be extinguiſhed, and the kingdom fall again into confuſion.

At laſt, however, it was mutually agreed, that all accounts ſhould be examined; and that whatever deficiencies appeared, the King ſhould immediately diſcharge them, on the Prince taking the matter to himſelf, on receiving proper ſecurity from the King; and if he deſired the men at arms to remain in Caſtile, he ſhould aſſign over twenty caſtles in his kingdom, at the nomination of the Prince, as a pledge for the payment of thoſe troops.

Peter replied, that he was very willing to inveſt the Prince with the lordſhip of Biſcay; but for his ſoldiers, he did not want them; and as to the twenty caſtles, he could not give an anſwer, as he would firſt ſee what arrears remained due.

Upon this ſir John Chandos was ordered by the Prince to draw out a complete ſtatement of the ſums diſburſed for the King of Caſtile, for the troops; which amounting to a large ſum, made the Prince more preſſing for the delivery of the caſtles before-mentioned. Sir John Chandos

dos alſo renewed his claim for a grant of the city of Soria in Caſtile, which had been promiſed him.

The King demurred ſtrongly reſpecting the caſtles; adding, that he could not think of conſenting to ſuch a requeſt; for what would his ſubjects ſay, to ſee ſo many places mortgaged, and delivered over to foreigners; which would alienate their affections, and occaſion a revolt: That for the city of Soria, he was ready to grant it to ſir John Chandos, according to his promiſe.

The Prince now perceiving the ſtate of affairs, narrowed his claim to the ſums due; on which the King promiſed to ſend diſpatches all over his kingdom to raiſe the monies neceſſary, and that as faſt as they were paid into his exchequer, the Prince ſhould be ſatisfied: mean time that his three daughters ſhould remain as hoſtages at Bayonne, till the balance was paid.

All this being agreed to, the King ordered the proper letters to be made out, inveſting the Prince of Wales with the lordſhip of Biſcay, who ſent two of his council, the lord of Povanne, and the chief-juſtice of Bordeaux, to receive the inveſti-

tture;

ture; the King ſending at the ſame time Fernan Perez de Ayala into Biſcay, as his commiſſioner for that purpoſe; who managed matters ſo well, according to his private inſtructions, that the Biſcayans unanimouſly refuſed to accept the Prince of Wales for their lord; though ever after, in all public deeds, ſubſequent to his other titles, the Prince conſtantly ſtiled himſelf Lord of Biſcay (L). But here the matter ended, and he was fairly duped out of that grant.

Sir John Chandos was ſerved much in the ſame manner; for when he claimed the King's grant of the city of Soria, the chancellor of Caſtile demanded ten thouſand doblas for the fee of inveſtiture, which extravagant ſum Chandos conſidered as a refuſal, and gave up the point.

Such were the rewards to theſe valiant Engliſhmen for reſtoring the King of Caſtile to the poſſeſſion of his throne.

The Prince of Wales now began to perceive what little dependence there was on his Caſtilian ally; however, his magnanimous mind, ſtill ſuperior to every diſappointment, induced him to ſhew the King the difference of his own conduct from that of his couſin of Spain, of which he now experienced ſo ungrateful a ſpecimen. He therefore propoſed to Peter, as he did not mean to avail himſelf of his immediate ſituation, and at the ſame time to put his honour to the teſt, that in final ſettlement of all dependencies, they ſhould both meet publicly in the cathedral of Burgos, where the King ſhould ſwear, on the Holy Evangeliſts, to fulfil all agreements; and that the Prince, rather than leave him abruptly to the mercy of his rebellious ſubjects, would ſtay four months longer in Caſtile.

THIS being aſſented to, one of the gates of the city of Burgos was ceded to the Prince, as a ſecurity, where he might place one thouſand men at arms and a body of archers.

THEN the Prince of Wales, unarmed, mounted on a beautiful courſer, attended by the duke of Lancaſter and a courtly train of Engliſh knights, made his entry into the city of Burgos, and rode to the cathedral, where he was met by Peter, ſurrounded by many lords of his Court; in whoſe preſence, and that of an immenſe croud of ſpectators, the Caſtilian monarch in an audible voice ſwore

ſwore on the Croſs and on the Holy Evangeliſts, that he ſtood indebted to the illuſtrious Prince of Wales, and his army, for the ſums then mentioned: and inaſmuch as he was not then in a condition to pay the ſame, he ſolemnly promiſed, in virtue of his oath, to diſcharge one moiety thereof in his realm of Caſtile, in the term of four months; and the remainder in the city of Bayonne, at the expiration of twelve months; that in the interval the three Infanta's his daughters ſhould remain as hoſtages in Bayonne. The King alſo ſwore, in the ſame manner, to inveſt the Prince with the lordſhip of Biſcay, and ſir John Chandos with the city of Soria; after which auguſt ceremony Peter returned to his palace, and the Prince of Wales to his reſidence at Las Huelgas.

A few days after, the King waited on the Prince, and told him he would make a progreſs in his kingdom, and go to the city of Seville, and collect all the monies himſelf, in order to make the payments ſtipulated; for which the Prince thanked him, and recommended the ſame to his attention, in conſideration of the ſignal ſervices that had been rendered to him; ſlightly hinting the reports that had been ſpread, of his having ſent private inſtructions to prevent the Biſcayans

 from

from receiving him as their lord, which he would not give credit to; and pressing Peter to give him possession thereof, as well as sir John Chandos of the city of Soria. To this the King replied, that he had never given any such instructions, and was willing to confer those grants as required; that in the course of four months he would take care that every thing promised should be fulfilled.

After this interview, the King took leave of the Prince of Wales, and set out for Aranda de Duero, while the Prince removed to Valladolid, with an intention of remaining in Castile the four months stipulated to close all dependencies with the King before his return to Guyenne, where his presence became every day more necessary, as well on account of the disturbances arisen during his absence, as for the recovery of his health, which had been much impaired since his arrival in Castile; the air of which did not agree with his constitution, no more than with the troops, many of whom had been carried off by fluxes, owing to intemperance; or from the usual distempers incident to the change of climate, and military fatigues.

CHAP-

CHAPTER THE FIFTH.

Peter returns to Seville—Puts to death the Lady Osorio, Mother of Alfonso de Guzman.—The Prince of Wales, after sending three English Knights to Seville, returns to Guyenne.—His Death.

THE great renown of the Prince of Wales and the valour of the English had struck such a terror into the Castilians, that where-ever Peter appeared, his authority became in full force. But alas! a power supported merely by a foreign aid, could only be momentary, and not answer the great purposes of government; which undoubtedly tend to the benefit of the governed, as well as the governor, founded on those mutual and reciprocal ties by which mankind are formed into civil compact and rational society; the truth of which the unhappy monarch whose life we are now writing woefully experienced.

THOUGH this ill-fated sovereign received intelligence that the bastard Henry had survived his late defeat, and had taken refuge in Aragon, yet he still vainly flattered himself, that after the signal victory of Nagera all opposition was totally broken, and every ſpark of rebellion extinguiſhed. This led him, inſtead of tempering the ferment of the times with the healing gifts of moderation and clemency, to perſevere againſt thoſe who fell under the weight of his diſpleaſure.

THUS, in paſſing through the cities of Toledo and Cordova, freſh acts of rigour took place. This latter city, in particular, was thrown into the utmoſt conſternation by his preſence. The inhabitants had ſhewn a decided partiality to Henry, and now found themſelves ſubject to the caprice of two rivals ſucceſſively; one moment expoſed to the ſeverity of Peter, the next dreading the reſentment of Henry.

PETER, attended by a few armed men, is ſaid to have one night perambulated the ſtreets of the city of Cordova, and to have entered ſeveral houſes, where he put ſixteen citizens to death, who had been active againſt him during his reſidence in Guyenne.

THE citizens of Seville, on the approach of Peter, found themſelves obliged to relinquiſh their new ſyſtem of politics, and return again to the obedience of their ſovereign. To ingratiate themſelves once more in his favour, the firſt ſtep of the magiſ-

trates

trates was to imprison all those of Henry's party who had not been fortunate enough to make their escape. Of this number were the high-admiral Boccanegra (M), and Ponze de Leon lord of Marchena, who were soon after put to death in due form of law by the officers of Peter.

As to Boccanegra and Ponze de Leon, it cannot be denied but that they were found in a state of rebellion, and would have suffered a similar punishment in any kingdom of Europe at the time. The ungrateful Boccanegra was more remarkably reprehensible, as the late king Alfonso had settled good estates on his family, as well out of regard to his brother Simon doge of Genoa, as from his naval abilities; for which reason he had been made high-admiral of Castile, and Peter had given him the command of his fleet.

The fate of the two admirals of Castile and of Aragon was remarkable. Boccanegra, from a private citizen in a mercantile republic, after being raised to high dignities in the kingdom of Castile, and honours intailed on his family, finished his days ingloriously; and Bernal viscount de Cabrera, the admiral of Aragon, whose naval services were likewise eminent in a ſupreme degree, loſt his popularity in the cabinet, and equally met with a deplorable fate.

The King appeared again in wrath, in his favourite palace of Seville, whoſe gardens and ſhady bowers were once the ſeat of his amours with the lovely Padilla, and its cool receſſes the pleaſing retreat from the ſcorching heats of ſummer. But nature had not endowed the heart of Peter with benevolent ſenſations: the hours of dalliance were rapidly ſucceeded by guſts of violence and paſſion. The fond Padilla had often attempted to ſoothe and lull theſe fatal convulſions; but ſhe was now no more, and Peter's vengeance, bereft of that tender mediatrix, no longer knew any bounds, and he fell on the fair-ſex without mercy.

The very name of Guzman was hateful to him; the more, as ſo many individuals of that family had been ſtrenuous in ſupport of the ſons of Leonora. Among the reſt, that ancient and reſpectable perſonage the lady Oſorio, mother of Don John Alfonſo de Guzman, having eſpouſed the cabals of her ſon, became the firſt victim to the reſentment of the monarch after his return to Seville. Her ſon

ſon had made his eſcape; but this unhappy lady was ſeized, and ordered to be burnt in a public ſquare in that city.

THIS tragic ſcene afforded a moſt tender and affectionate inſtance of the fondneſs and attachment of Spaniſh women, in the perſon of Iſabella Davalos, attendant on the lady Oſorio; who, in this fatal moment, perceiving the perſon of her venerable protectreſs expoſed to the wind, impetuouſly ruſhed forward to compoſe her garments, and periſhed with her in the flames. For this act of tender regard, the family of Guzman have entailed a charge on their heirs for ever, not to refuſe relief to whomſoever of the name of Davalos ſhould ever apply for it, enjoining every malediction on ſuch as refuſed it. The friends of the family of Guzman collected the aſhes of this unfortunate lady and her incomparable handmaid; and they were depoſited in a ſumptuous monument (N).

THE next who ſuffered was the late Treaſurer Yanez, who, not ſatisfied with remaining a priſoner at Seville, had taken up arms, and appeared againſt his maſter at the battle of Nagera. He was afterwards apprehended in Aſturias, and brought to Seville, where he was legally convicted, and ſuffered

fered a condign punifhment for his conduct (O).

THE Prince of Wales remained all this time in Valladolid, impatiently expecting the return of the King, or, at leaft, fome tidings from his Treafurers, according to agreement; but waiting in vain till the feaft of St. John Baptift, when the weather became intolerably fuffocating and hot, he difpatched three of his knights to Seville, fir William Loring, fir Richard Ponchardon, and fir Thomas Bannifter, to remind the King of his promifes, and haften the conclufion thereof.

THESE knights were courteoufly received by the King; but when they entered on the purport of their miffion, the fovereign made a variety of excufes; affuring them he was infinitely difpleafed that he had not punctually performed his engagements with the Prince, the particulars of which he had frequently urged to his fubjects, who pleaded their inability to raife fuch confiderable fums while the Companions were in arms in his kingdom, by whom his minifters, difpatched to the Prince, had been more than once plundered: he therefore defired they would inform their mafter, that it was his earneft requeft

he

he would pleafe to withdraw his armed men out of the realm, efpecially thofe rude foldiers termed the Companions, and leave a chofen band of Englifh knights, to whom he would undoubtedly pay the fums of money for which he ftood engaged; that is, one moiety of the pay due to the army, in four months from the date agreed on; and the remainder in the twelvemonth enfuing.

THIS being all the fatisfaction the Englifh knights could obtain from the King of Caftile, they returned to Valladolid, where they found the Prince of Wales much indifpofed, and the troops in a very fickly condition, from the great heats of fummer: the Prince moreover being highly difgufted with the treatment he had received, fully determined to quit the country and return to Guyenne. Having therefore ranfomed the lord D'Andregam, the Begue de Villaine (P) and others, in exchange for fir Hugh Haftings and other Englifh knights, he quitted Valladolid, and returned through Navarre to Guyenne. But finding his indifpofition daily encreafing he went back to England, where this excellent prince departed this life in his palace of Weftminfter, in the forty-fixth year of his age, and ended a career of glory, with the admiration of all Europe.

It was reported, according to Walſingham, that the Prince died of poiſon; but if we conſider the great fatigue of this expedition, commenced in a moſt ſevere and inclement ſeaſon, ſucceeded by the violent heats and intemperate air of Caſtile, candour muſt add, that ſomething more than report is expected, when we are to give credit to ſuch an aſſertion, in contradiction to which ſo many natural cauſes occurred to occaſion the event.

Having ſaid ſo much of the Prince of Wales, I cannot take leave of this ſubject without paying a juſt tribute to the memory of an illuſtrious Spaniard, who was not only his cotemporary, but ſingularly attached to his perſon, and to the Engliſh nation in general. This was Don Sancho Martinez de Leyva, ſon of Don John Martinez de Leyva, firſt lord of the bed-chamber to king Alfonſo XI. and *Adelantado Mayor* of Caſtile. His ſon Sancho came over to England, where he offered his ſervices to Edward III. and attended on John duke of Lancaſter in his expedition to Scotland. He afterwards went into France, and ſerved under the Prince of Wales, with whom he was at the famous battle and victory of Poictiers. After this he commanded the Engliſh army in Picardy,

Picardy, and was very inſtrumental in the advantages gained over the French in thoſe wars; and from his remarkable ſtrength of body was called *Brazo de fierro*, or "Iron Arm." In recompence for his ſervices, when he returned to England, Edward III. to teſtify his regard for his perſon, gave him in marriage his natural daughter Elizabeth, by Elizabeth Suffolk, counteſs of Northumberland, granting him further the privilege, in addition to his paternal coat armour, to quarter the armorial bearings of England (Q).

CHAPTER THE SIXTH.

Henry arrives safe in Aragon.—The King of Navarre extricates himself by a new Stratagem out of the Hands of Sir Oliver Manny.—Henry is well received by the Duke of Anjou at Montpellier, and supported by France, prepares for a second Invasion of Castile.

THE affairs of the Bastard seemed now to be desperate in the extreme. Peter held the reins of government in Seville, and his enemies were dispersed. Henry after the battle of Nagera had made a precipitate flight into Aragon, and narrowly escaped a surprise on the road by a party of Peter's soldiers, from whom he extricated himself by his valour, killing the person who endeavoured to take him, and then got safe into Aragon; where meeting, at a village near Calatayud, with Don Pedro de Luna, afterwards the celebrated antipope Benedict XIII. he conducted him through Aragon to the Count de Foix, who, though not overpleased to see him, nor to give umbrage to the Prince of Wales, furnished him with money and horses to continue his journey.

At

At Montpellier the Baftard was well received by the duke of Anjou, governor of Languedoc, as well as by pope Urban V. at Avignon, who favoured his caufe in private, though, with the ufual policy of that court, avoiding as much as poffible to give jealoufy to the King of England, from whom he met with that reverence with which his pontifical character was univerfally held amongft chriftian princes ; but with refpect to the interference and conduct of the cardinals who compofed it, in favour of Henry, we fhall not have a favourable opinion of their rectitude, if any credit is given to the letters of Petrarch, who, as an eye-witnefs, has given in the moft glaring colours a ftriking picture of their manners.

The fugitive Henry feemed neverthelefs to be in a forlorn condition ; his foreign friends were awed by the Englifh, and thofe in Caftile were depreffed by King Peter, who was ftill fupported by the Prince. As the councils of Henry were diftracted ; each party endeavoured to make up his differences as well as he was able.

None ftood in a more precarious fituation at this juncture than Charles king of Navarre, who had

had treated with both fides, fully determined to abide by the ftrongeft; and now the time drew near to play off the final game of his politics. It has been related with what art he prevailed on fir Oliver Manny to feize his perfon, to prevent his appearing in battle with the Prince of Wales; for which fervice he had promifed Manny to fettle on him an eftate in Normandy, which belonged to the king of Navarre, and a yearly income of three thoufand francs of gold. He now engaged Manny to reconduct him to the city of Tudela in his own dominions, offering to leave his fecond fon at Borja, as hoftage for what he had promifed.—The Infante Don Peter of Navarre was fent to Borja, and the credulous Manny conveyed the king to the city of Tudela; but when Charles found himfelf once more in his own dominions, he put Manny in prifon, whofe brother loft his life in endeavouring to make his efcape. The king refufed to releafe Manny till the Infante was fent back; and Manny was glad to fave his life and return home without his caftle in Normandy, or the penfion promifed by the king; who, finding the face of affairs changed, paid fedulous court to the Prince of Wales's intereft, and by every ftratagem and artifice accommodated himfelf to the fituation of the times; by which, not

without

without reafon, he acquired the title of "Charles "the Wicked."

THE king of Aragon fhewed himfelf no lefs verfed in political fpeculation, and exhibited the little to be expected from the great, when their intereft does not clofely coincide with their profeffions. The enterprizing Henry, though proclaimed king of Caftile by the free confent of the people, had to his coft experienced this leffon. This gallant foldier, beloved in Caftile, and in univerfal efteem with the Aragoneze nation, was now mortified with reproaches from that crown. The king refufed his daughter the Infanta Leonora in marriage with his fon Don John, and upbraided him with breach of promife, after he had been proclaimed king of Caftile.

To perplex Henry ftill more, he beheld the king of Aragon liften to the advances of the Prince of Wales and King Peter, who proffered new treaties of alliance, to detach him finally from the Baftard. Sir Hugh de Calverley was fent into Aragon on this commiffion, as an able negotiator, who, having ferved long in Spain, was well acquainted with the manners and genius of the

 people;

people; for in thofe days it was the cuftom of the Englifh, when minifters were fent to foreign courts, always to employ fuch as were verfed in the language and cuftoms of thofe, to whom they were fent.

HENRY was greatly embarraffed by thefe negotiations; his dejected family remained at Saragoffa, not knowing where to retire for fhelter or protection.

MEAN-TIME the court of Aragon had alfo its inteftine divifions, and was fplit into parties. The principal one, the court party, were for treating with King Peter, and fettling all their differences with Caftile, to retrieve their country by agriculture, and treaties of commerce, on a bafis of reciprocity; adding, that Henry had engaged them in an expenfive war, without making good his engagements, and diftreffed their finances to a very great degree. Of this party were the count of Urgel, the count of Cardona, and the bifhop of Lerida, who were the principal minifters of the cabinet. On the other hand, the oppofition was clamorous in favour of Henry, as a counterpoife to the enterprifing fpirit of Peter. Confidering Caftile as a natural enemy to their kingdom, they

reprefented

reprefented that the Baftard fhould be fupported as a pretender to the crown; which, by difuniting the people, would make a powerful diverfion, and be finally advantageous by weakening the power and refources of the enemy. Of this party were the Infante Don Peter of Aragon, uncle to the king; De Luna, archbifhop of Saragoffa; and the count of Ampurias, with fome others.—— This party were a decided minority; but they had fome good fpeakers, and men of great oratorical powers, who held the Cortes a long time in fufpence by the brilliancy of their genius, and lively fallies of wit, fupported by integrity of character, and purity of fentiment, that did infinite honour; fhewing at the fame time the early ftate of literature in that kingdom, and a fuperiority of genius over the grave Caftilians, who flighted foreign improvement, while their more lively neighbours the Aragonefe courted the Mufes, and imitated the poetic numbers of Italy, ftrewing flowers even in the fenate, over the moft ferious fubjects, and enlivening languid debate with picturefque colours, in order to obtain a ferious ear to the diftreffes of their country. A third party had fprung up, who wifhed for peace with Caftile at all events; and that it might be brought about by lenient meaſures, without going to extremities, and involving the kingdom in foreign wars.

WHILE debates ran high in the councils of Aragon, Henry, finding his intereſt in the wain in that kingdom, endeavoured to enter into new negotiations with the duke of Anjou, though this did not afford any great proſpect. England and France being at peace at that juncture, his hopes were not very great, and a character of ſuch enterprize as Henry was rather an unwelcome gueſt at that period: however, as the court of France are ever watchful of political events, and generally purſue one fixed point undiſturbed by political cabal or courtly intrigue; it was fortunate for Henry, that it ſeemed expedient at all events, to give him encouragement in oppoſition to the allies of England, to weaken the reſources of that powerful ſtate, and prevent their reaping the benefits of a peace of any duration.

THE character of Peter was moreover ſo odious in France, from his behaviour to queen Blanche of Bourbon, that any meaſure againſt him with the leaſt plauſible aſpect, was ſure to become popular, and acceptable to a nation naturally

naturally fond of their monarch, and every branch of his houſe. The propoſals of Henry were therefore liſtened to, and orders ſent by Charles to his brother the duke of Anjou, to pay to Henry fifty thouſand florins in gold, and aſſign him the county of Ceſanon for himſelf and his family. The count of Anjou alſo added fifty thouſand florins more from himſelf. Henry now began to purchaſe horſes and arms, was joined by many of his friends, and his affairs once more ſeemed to take a more favourable turn.

These tidings no ſooner reached Caſtile than many reſorted to him, as well as numerous adventurers from France. Henry then prevailed on the duke of Anjou to ſend meſſengers to the court of Aragon, appriſing the king of the favourable manner in which his affairs were conſidered in France. By theſe he wrote preſſing letters to the king of Aragon, inviting him to join him; but they were treated with ſilence and ſlight: however, his party daily gained ground, and he learned with great pleaſure, that all the priſoners taken at the battle of Nagera were ſet at liberty, and returned to their eſtates; that Guzman had made good his retreat from Seville, and was zealous to appear in his ſupport whenever a good opportunity offered: that the cities of Segovia, Valladolid, Placentia, and ſome others in Caſtile had declared for him, as well as Biſcay, and all the province of Guypuſcoa, except the ſea-ports of St. Sebaſtian's and Guetaria.

The Baſtard learned moreover, that diſturbances had ariſen in Guyenne, which foreboded a rupture between England and France; all which brightened his proſpects, and ſeemed the forerunners of his future greatneſs. He further learned that the Prince of Wales, after waiting the four months agreed on at Valladolid, and receiving no money from the King, had quitted Spain in diſguſt, along with the troops, who ravaged Caſtile in their march, and made a deſert of the kingdom.

Matters being come to this criſis, Henry concluded a new treaty of alliance with France, and prepared himſelf for a ſubſequent and more ſucceſsful invaſion of Caſtile. Many of his friends taken priſoners at the battle of Nagera now joined him, with foreigners from all parts; but of all the military adventurers who followed the fortunes of Henry in Spain, none

were

were more conſpicuous or ſucceſsful than the baſtard de Bearne, a young ſoldier of great expectation, and baſe ſon of Gaſton Phœbus, count of Foix, and lord of Bearne. Through the intereſt of Henry, this ſplendid ſoldier had the good fortune to marry the lady Iſabella Lacerda, a rich widow, and ſiſter to Don John de la Cerda, who had been put to death in Seville for rebellion. On this marriage De Bearne was created Count of Medina-Celi by Henry, and became founder of one of the firſt ducal houſes in the kingdom, with an immenſe eſtate, which his deſcendants enjoy to this day (R).

CHAPTER THE SEVENTH.

Civil State of the Kingdom of Aragon. Definition of the Cortes of the Province of Catalonia.

IF we for a moment turn our eyes on the kingdom of Aragon, examine the political and civil ſtate of that country, and view with attention their love of liberty; we ſhall not be ſurpriſed at the freedom of debate which animated their councils, and gave riſe to that brilliancy of ſentiment and expreſſion, which broke forth in the aſſembly of the Cortes, and leaned with ſuch partiality in favour of Henry; though the court party weighed down every effort, and left the Baſtard to depend upon the private aſſiſtance of his friends.

THE Aragoneſe were a ſprightly warlike people, who united the love of letters to that of liberty and honour. At an early period their lively genius made them emulous of their neighbours in Languedoc; and their fondneſs for poetic compoſition was not leſs conſpicuous than amongſt thoſe famous Troubadours, who made ſuch a figure

figure under the reign of the first counts of Toulouse (S).

WITH respect to their love of civil liberty, it was clearly evinced by the tribunal of the *Justiza*, one of the greatest efforts of liberty known at that time on the Continent. The Cortes of the kingdom also varied in many respects from those assemblies held in Castile. Having defined the former, I shall at present annex the mode of holding the Cortes in the province of Catalonia, in presence of the king of Aragon, inasmuch as it illustrates the legislation of Aragon, and forms a delineation of the manners and customs of the times under present consideration; shewing the administration of an heroic nation, long the rival of Castile, not less brave or worthy; fallen since under their dominion, as a sister kingdom, united in the same ties of amity, prosperity, and glory.

THIS assembly, which represented the legislative government of the Province of Catalonia, was composed of the clergy, lords, and commons, of that extensive domain.

THE

The clergy were represented by the archbishop of Taragona as president, with the bishops of Barcelona, Girona, Lerida, Tortosa, Urgel, Vique, Solsona, and Elna, with deputies from the cathedral chapters; the castellan of Ampurias, prior of Catalonia; the knights commandeurs of St. John of Jerusalem; with the mitred abbots holding estates *cum mero et mixto imperio.*

The nobility consisted of the duke of Cardona as president, with all the earls, marquisses, viscounts, barons, knights, and esquires, of the province.

The commons consisted of the representatives of the cities of Barcelona, Lerida, Girona, Tortosa, Vique, Cervera, Montesa, Balaguer, Perpignan, with twenty-four towns or boroughs who had votes in the Cortes.

The Cortes were summoned by the king's writ directed to the presidents of the three estates, in which the king nominated the place and day of assembling.

If any member of the Cortes was prevented by illness from attending, he might name a proxy.

The

THE form of the king's writ to the three eſtates was ſimilar, with this difference only; to the clergy the king ſaid, *Rogamus et monemus*; but to the lords and commons he ſaid, *Vobis dicimus et mandamus*.

IF by inadvertency any of the Cortes happened to be excluded, there was a nullity in all the proceedings.

IF the king could not attend on account of illneſs or abſence from the kingdom, the hereditary prince as heir apparent might ſummons the Cortes, being properly authorized by the ſovereign, with the conſent of the Cortes.

THE king might nominate the place of holding the Cortes, provided it was ſituated in the province, and was a town of at leaſt two hundred houſes.

THE king might further alter the place appointed for the aſſembly of the Cortes, provided ſuch alteration was made previous to their meeting. After they were once aſſembled, no change could be effected without the conſent of the three eſtates.

The king was to appear in perſon in the Cortes. However, he had forty days allowed him; meantime the Cortes might ſit and prorogue their ſeſſions, in the king's name, by commiſſion.

In caſe of the king's illneſs, the Cortes might be convened in the palace of the ſovereign, or in his private apartments, by means of deputies from the three eſtates.

The king opened the ſeſſions by a ſpeech from the throne directed to the three eſtates; to which they returned an anſwer ſuitable to the ſolemn form in which they were addreſſed.

None were admitted near the throne but the heir apparent and the lord high chamberlain with the *Eſtoque*, (poignard of ſtate) as a badge of his office.

After the ſeſſion was opened, a committee of eighteen perſons were choſen, of which nine were on the part of the king, and nine for the eſtates; that is, three members for each eſtate. Theſe were termed *Habilitadores*, or Scrutineers. They examined the qualifications of the members; had a right to reject ſuch as were not properly qualified; and their deciſions were final, without any further

further appeal. Thoſe who appeared for the king were ſeated on his right hand, and the others on the left. They all took the oaths of fealty and homage to the king.

THREE commiſſioners were appointed on the part of the king, who were generally grandees, and termed *Tratadores*. They propoſed the buſineſs in the king's name to the eſtates, and conferred with them thereupon.

ANOTHER committee of eighteen perſons were appointed to take cognizance of all breaches of charter, and of debts contracted in the king's name: they paſſed ſentence in a ſummary way in all caſes of infringements of the conſtitution, or irregularities of the officers or miniſters of the crown. Of this court nine were for the king, and nine for the ſubject. They were termed in the Catalonian dialect, *Judges de Greuges*; ſimilar to an office in France, named *Juges des Griefs*.

THIS committee was veſted with full powers from the king, with conſent of the Cortes, to judge fairly and candidly of all grievances and injuries done to the eſtates of the Cortes at large.

THEY

THEY continued fitting during ten months after the Cortes were diffolved, to fubftantiate their proceedings, and held their meetings in the city of Barcelona.

WHEN the Cortes were fitting, the general chamber of revenue delivered to each prefident of the three eftates the filver mace, and then the powers of the chambers were in fufpence.

ALL the members of the Cortes were feated, and were to fpeak in the Catalonian dialect.

NONE but natives of the province could have feats and votes in the Cortes; but foreigners holding fiefs or lordfhips in the province, might appear there as barons.

THE king could not prolong the time of appearance for abfentees cited by the Cortes, unlefs at their own defire, as this depended upon their determination.

No gentleman could fit in the Cortes before he was twenty years of age. If he was infolvent for public monies received, he was excluded when the debt proceeded from his own mifconduct; but if merely

merely from the failure of the tenant, it did not then deprive him of his feat.

Though the members of the Cortes had full powers from their conftituents for the bufinefs of the province, they were to have a fpecial authority to fwear in the heir apparent to the Crown.

The members muft be natives of the province; proxies were only admiffible in cafes of illnefs; no abfentees could appoint proxies, unlefs fuch abfence was on the bufinefs of the ftate

In the power given to proxies the claufe muft be fpecially expreffed, giving power to vote and grant the fupplies for the national purpofes.

Such as abfented themfelves without leave, could never be re-admitted into the Cortes.

The reprefentatives on the part of the lords were, of courfe, of that body. For the commons, he muft be a member of one of their municipal courts, and dwelling in the place that he reprefented. The fame for the ecclefiaftical chapters.

One member could not reprefent two churches, two prelacies, or two baronies; but one gentleman might reprefent two or more of his degree. The commons might fend two or more members for one city; but they had only one vote.

The making new laws, and expounding or amending thofe already made, depended on the king, lords, and commons, in Cortes affembled, as well as all decifions relating to the incidental bufinefs of that affembly; but when any difagreement arofe between the three orders, and they did not concur in opinion, the power of fettling matters was vefted in the Crown.

The conftitution of the Province of Catalonia confifted in a charter in favour of the people reprefented by the Cortes, granted by Peter king of Aragon, in 1283, when the commons were admitted to fend reprefentatives for the cities and boroughs to fit with the clergy and nobility.

When the day came to clofe the feffions of the Cortes, or diffolve them, the king being feated on the throne, the prefident of the clergy rofe, and being uncovered, all the members likewife rofe and were uncovered: then the prefident read the refolutions resolutions that had passed, and supplicated the sovereign lord the king to swear to observe them. After this the president delivered this paper to the lord chancellor. The king rose, and walked to a table prepared for the purpose on his left hand, where, kneeling before a crucifix, and placing his right hand on the bible that lay open, the prothonotary, also kneeling, read aloud the oath tendered to his majesty, approving and confirming the acts and resolves of the Cortes. Then the king rose, made an obeisance before the crucifix, and returned to his throne. The act expressive of the grant was now read to his majesty: the prothonotary afterwards turning his face towards the assembly said aloud, "His majesty "permits the representatives of the Cortes to re-"turn home (T)."

CHAPTER THE EIGHTH.

Henry enters Castile.—Gets Possession of the Town of Calaborra.—Is also received in Burgos.—Lays Siege to Toledo.

WE now behold Henry, once more at the head of an army, preparing to return to Castile, where he was impatiently waited for by those turbulent lords who headed the powerful faction against Peter, whose clemency at the battle of Nagera had not in the least operated towards a reconciliation in his kingdom. On the contrary, they flew with new ardour to Henry, whose friends were in high spirits, ready to follow their leader; while the dejected Castilians were perplexed, on finding themselves deserted by the succours from England.

HENRY, to shew his confidence in the success of this new enterprize, took with him his Countess and his son Don John; and having marshalled his troops, and represented to them his determined resolution

resolution to repossess himself of his kingdom, he began his march towards Castile.

On the other hand, the king of Aragon no sooner heard of his motions, than he sent the governour of Roussillon to request that he would not pass through his territories, which would give umbrage to his ally the Prince of Wales, and that he should be obliged to oppose his passage.

The Bastard received this intimation with becoming spirit; and told the governor he was much surprised that the king should send such a message, knowing so well the services he had rendered; having obtained for him, at one irruption into Castile, no less than twenty towns and as many castles: that he could not avoid passing through his territories, and, if he thought proper to oppose him, he might use his pleasure; as on his part he should oppose force to force, and fight his way forward. This, notwithstanding the difficulties he encountered, being constantly harrassed by detachments from Aragon, he nevertheless effected, as they never ventured to attack him in the open field, knowing the undaunted resolution of their antagonist.

In the county of Ribargoſſa, belonging to the Infante Don Pedro of Aragon, head of the oppoſition in his favour, he was amply ſupplied with proviſions, and met by that prince at Barabara, who provided him with guides, and was very inſtrumental in the ſucceſs of that expedition. At Balbaſtro he learned that the king of Aragon was at Saragoſſa, and had given orders to intercept him; but Henry having many friends in that country, had the good fortune to paſs without oppoſition, and entered on the territory of Caſtile.

He no ſooner found himſelf once more in that kingdom, than he drew out his impatient army in order of battle on the banks of the Ebro. Here, diſmounting his horſe, at the head of the troops he drew his ſword, and kneeling on one knee made a croſs with the point of his ſword on the ſand; then ſolemnly ſwore by that croſs, that he never would quit the kingdom of Caſtile in queſt of foreign ſuccour, but live or die with thoſe valiant knights now with him, and would ſhare with them the fate of the event.

He next conferred the honour of knighthood on the baſtard de Bearne, and on a French eſquire of the name of Talbot, recommended to him by the

count

count de Foix, at whofe houfe he had feen him after the defeat at Nagera.

HENRY now put his army in motion, and marched joyfully forward to the city of Calahorra, where, on a former occafion, he had been firft proclaimed king of Caftile. Here many Caftilians joined him, who had been with him at Nagera; amongft the reft Don Gomez Manrique, archbifhop of Toledo, whofe venerable prefence was of great fervice, as the appearance of fo illuftrious a prelate had great influence over the people.

HENRY finding himfelf thus countenanced, determined to pufh boldly forward, in order to correfpond with the zeal of his adherents. With this view he marched to the city of Logrono; but thofe loyal Caftilians, conftant and fteady to their fovereign, fhut the gates againft him. On this he wheeled about, and moved towards Burgos, fending fcouts to difcover the fentiments of the citizens. Thofe fickle people expreffed their readinefs to receive the baftard Henry, but were overawed by the governor, who held the city for King Peter. However, Henry approached nearer, to avail himfelf of any favourable circumftance.

He no ſooner appeared in ſight of the city, than the biſhop, at the head of the clergy, with many citizens came out to meet him; but the brave governor, Alonſo Hernandez, retired into the citadel with the troops, where he held out for his ſovereign King Peter, and kept firing on the city. Henry, however, having undermined him, he was obliged, not receiving any ſuccour, to ſurrender on capitulation, by which Henry once more got poſſeſſion of the important city of Burgos. Here he found his brother-in-law Don Philip de Caſtro, taken priſoner at the battle of Nagera, whom he ſet at liberty, and ſettled a fair eſtate on him in Caſtile, as he did on many others of his followers, as well foreigners as Caſtilians. Such was the reputation of his bounty, that every foreigner at his return home boaſted of his caſtles in Spain; which ſoon became a proverbial expreſſion in France to denote imaginary poſſeſſions; and remains a colloquial idiom of that language to this day.

The court of Henry was eſtabliſhed at Burgos, where he enjoyed every outward mark of royalty, in addition to the voice of a numerous people, who had made a ſettlement of the Crown in his favour, as a perſon endowed with thoſe virtues

virtues requisite to protect them in their liberties. As a further encouragement to these spirited efforts in defence of their injured rights, Henry received the pleasing news that the city of Cordova had revolted, and declared for him: that King Peter was in Seville, which still acknowledged his sovereignty; though numbers of his subjects, in the remote parts of Castile, had sided with Henry.

The better to give countenance to his party, he kept his army in motion; and having sent his family to Ilescas near Toledo, with the archbishop of that see he proceeded to the town of Duenas, where they were in force for King Peter, and impeded his march, preventing him from getting to Valladolid. However, after a month's siege, the garrison of Duenas receiving no succours, were obliged to submit, and surrendered to Henry.

In the month of January following, the active Henry marched into the kingdom of Leon, whose capital surrendered, with great part of the kingdom, as did that of Asturias. Thus the greatest part of the monarchy acknowledged the benevolent Henry; while Peter was, in a manner, shut up in his capital of Seville, possessing only some part of Andalusia, and the loyal kingdom of Murcia, which retained its fidelity to the last.

HENRY, anxious to bring on a final engagement, called a council, to advise what measures were best to be followed at this important moment. Some were for marching directly to Seville, to attack the King, and avail themselves of the popular enthusiasm; but being in want of money and provisions necessary for so long a march, it was judged more prudent to maintain themselves in Castile, and to invest the city of Toledo. This plan was therefore adopted In the mean time. they seized on the town of Madrid (V), and some others in that district; after which Henry marched towards the city of Toledo. That place was well provided with troops, under that veteran soldier Fernan Alvarez de Toledo, firmly attached to the King, and determined to defend the city to the last extremity. The besiegers, on their part, carried on the attack with no less spirit, but were as vigorously opposed by the garrison; so that the operations became tedious, and augured little prospect of success; though the besiegers neglected no means to carry the place, and had thrown a bridge over the Tagus, and detached a considerable body to take post on the other side

of

of the river: but all was in vain; the loyalty of the citizens was not to be shaken.

Henry for the first time sent orders to the mint at Burgos to coin money in his name; which were called *Sesenas*, from their being of the value of six pennies. To compensate for the disappointment arising from the obstinate defence of the besieged, other events happened which made amends for this procrastination. While Henry lay before Toledo, ambassadors arrived at his camp from Charles VI. of France, who sent his chamberlain Francis de Perelles, viscount de Rhodez, and John de Ric, lord of Neburis, to acquaint him that war was declared between England and France, and offering a closer alliance with Henry, with promises to support him with all his power; in proof of which, reinforcements should soon be sent to him, under the command of De Guesclin.

Great rejoicings took place in Henry's camp at this agreeable news, and the most vigorous measures were immediately devised. The siege of Toledo had now lasted eighteen months to very little purpose. The brave citizens, seconding the valour of the troops, persisted in their resolution to die

die under its walls with that heroiſm which ſo often diſtinguiſhed the Caſtilians.

THEIR courage and loyalty at laſt rouſed Peter from his lethargy; he determined to come to their ſuccour, and once more boldly ſtand forward in defence of his tottering kingdom.

CHAP-

CHAPTER THE NINTH.

King Peter invites the King of Granada to join him.—Lays Siege to the City of Cordova.—The Infidels destroy the Country.—Peter marches against the Bastard Henry.—Is defeated on the Plains of Montiel.

THE affairs of King Peter bore at this juncture a most alarming aspect. A considerable army of the enemy had for a long time surrounded, and still continued the siege of Toledo, whose gallant defenders were almost exhausted with fatigue. To render their distress more feeling, they had the mortification to perceive that the French every day afforded new aid to the Bastard, and supported him openly against the King of Castile; whose dejected subjects, many of whom had hitherto continued inflexible in their fidelity, now seemed lukewarm in his interest, and ready to embrace the slightest pretext to throw off his authority.

THE adjacent districts in the environs of Seville were already in a state of revolt, under the influence

fluence of Guzman, who had escaped from Peter, and bore him an implacable hatred. The whole province of Andalusia soon adopted a similar propensity towards Henry. Mistrust, secret murmurings, and false reports, were spread every where, in which the fairest characters were attacked, and every ray of hope darkened. Even the loyal Martin Lope de Cordova, who had been with the King at Bayonne, was traduced, and near falling a victim to the jealousy of his enemies, if the king of Granada had not interfered, on hearing that he was arrested at Martos, by sending an express to the King, earnestly soliciting his release, or else that he would come in person with an army to effect it.

The whole kingdom was soon thrown into a state of anarchy. Those faithful cities in Castile, Logrono, Victoria, and Salvatierra, with some others of less note, which still held out for King Peter, now spent and exhausted, without ammunition or provisions, implored the King for aid and advice in their distress, since it was impossible for them to resist much longer against the repeated attacks of the Bastard, assisted by the French, who pressed on them on all sides; that sooner than fall off from their allegiance to their liege sovereign, they would prefer submitting to the king of Navarre,

varre, the ally of Caſtile, rather than ſurrender themſelves to any power that invaded their territories.

King Peter, equally jealous of the intrigues of the king of Navarre, thanked his loyal ſubjects for their attachment, and requeſted them to be of good cheer; that he would ſoon come to their relief; and recommended at the laſt extremity, rather than diſmember the monarchy, to yield to his baſe-brother Henry.

In this interval, however, the artful and ever-watchful king of Navarre had availed himſelf of the opportunity; and having ſeduced Don Tello de Caſtilla to detach himſelf from his brother Henry and join intereſts with him, they got poſſeſſion of thoſe cities juſt mentioned, which lay contiguous to the kingdom of Navarre; and they remained in that ſtate till other arrangements took place, and the king of Navarre found himſelf obliged to yield them again.

Peter now thought ſeriouſly of taking the field, though many of the inhabitants of Seville requeſted him to ſtay with them, and not expoſe his perſon to the inſidious deſigns of his enemies. But this Peter could not conſent to, and was determined

mined to oppofe them in the field. To ftrengthen his forces, he applied to his ally, Mahomet, king of Granada, requefting him to come to his affift-ance, who fent him feven thoufand horfe, and forty thoufand infantry. With this army, in addition to the Caftilian troops which Peter was able to mufter, he marched firft againft the city of Cordova, and with his infidel allies laid fiege to it. King Mahomet was in perfon along with his troops, and had got poffeffion of one of the principal towers. His foldiers behaved with the utmoft en-thufiafm, in hopes to recover that celebrated city, the pride of their religion; whofe beautiful mofque, now a chriftian church, had been for ages the object of their warmeft devotion. But all their fervour was vain againft the courage and valour of the befieged. The women appeared in the ftreets beating their breafts and tearing their hair, encouraging their countrymen to perfevere in their manly conduct, and refcue themfelves, their wives, and their children, from flavery and deftruction. The befieged, who were almoft fpent, were refolved to fell their lives dear; and, in one general attack, rufhed on the enemy with fuch violence, that the infidels were totally put to the rout, and obliged to retreat, as well as King Peter, who fwore in great wrath againft the city,

that

that if ever he reduced it to his obedience, he would ſet it on fire, and plough up the ground, to puniſh the inhabitants for their treaſon.

Soon after, Mahomet, in concert with Peter, led his troops againſt the city of Jaen, which he ſet fire to, ravaging its territory; after which theſe infidels extended themſelves as far as the city of Ubeda, which they deſtroyed in the ſame manner, as well as thoſe of Utrera and Marchena; carrying away eleven thouſand captives, including men women and children, who were reduced to a ſtate of the moſt abject ſlavery, and conveyed into the kingdom of Granada. Mahomet further recovered, and annexed once more to his dominion, thoſe towns and fortreſſes, which, on a former occaſion, he had been obliged to cede to King Peter, when he aſſiſted him againſt Rufus.

Thus on all ſides the dominions of the unhappy King of Caſtile were ravaged by fire and ſword; and ſuch were the fruits of his Mooriſh alliance, and of calling in a foreign power to defend his dominions.

Peter having thus laid waſte his fertile kingdom of Andaluſia, turned his thoughts to the relief

lief of the citizens of Toledo, and, previous to his departure, ſent his natural children, with his jewels and treaſure, to the city of Carmona, which he fortified, and made as ſtrong as poſſible. The king of Portugal alſo ſent him a body of men; and by the advice of Don Fernando de Caſtro, who never forſook him, he aſſembled a raw army, in addition to a body of Mooriſh horſe, and at the head of forty thouſand men marched towards Toledo, without waiting for ſir Hugh de Calverley, who was now coming to his aid with ſix thouſand men of the Companions, whom he had aſſembled in ſupport of the King.

Henry getting early intentions of the King's motions, as well as of his departure from Seville, was determined to give him battle the firſt opportunity that offered, and, if poſſible, by one general overthrow, to wreſt totally from him the kingdoms of Caſtile and Leon.

Having heard from deſerters that the citizens of Toledo were reduced to the utmoſt extremity, and had lived for many days on horſe-fleſh, though they ſtill defended themſelves with inflexible courage, Henry concluded they muſt ſoon

yield

yield through neceffity. To go in queft therefore of King Peter, he converted the fiege into a blockade, and left a body of men before it, under the command of Manrique archbifhop of Toledo, affifted by fome experienced officers. He then proceeded with the main body of his army to Orgaz, five leagues from Toledo, fending advice to his friends at Cordova of his defigns, and recommending them to follow the rear of King Peter.

At Orgaz Henry was joined by Don John Alfonfo de Gufman, and other lords from Andalufia under his influence: here he was alfo reinforced by De Guefclin with fix hundred lances from France. Flufhed with the moft fanguine expectations of victory, Henry addreffed himfelf to his foldiers, and, after exhorting them to be fteady, gave the command of the firft divifion of his army to De Guefclin, having under him Gufman, fupported by many lords of his kindred.

They foon learned from their fcouts, that King Peter's army was at no great diftance, cantoned in feparate bodies, without regularity, on the plains of Montiel.

On this intelligence, the intrepid Henry, in order to surprise the Castilians, made a forced march in the night, which being very dark they effected by means of torches; their valiant leader representing to his men that the moment was near at hand, and that this last effort would soon ease them from their toils, and give them free and quiet possession of the kingdom of Castile.

The governor of the castle of Montiel, Garcia Moran, an Asturian knight, no sooner perceived the light of these torches, than he sent word to Peter to be on his guard, as he apprehended the enemy were near. On this the King called in all his out-posts, and prepared for battle. This precipitate march of Henry had been effected with such celerity, that by day-break they came up with King Peter's army; and instantly the first division under De Guesclin began to engage, and soon drove back the advanced line of the Castilians, while the bastard Henry marched round to flank the main body, commanded by the King. A hot action took place, Peter shewing much resolution, exposing his person to every danger, with a sharp axe of massy steel in his hand, exerting himself with such extraordinary vigour that none could stand before him. The

Portugueze

Portugueze and the Moors alſo ſeconded Peter with great courage; but whether from want of diſcipline, or a proper command among ſuch different corps, the whole was ſoon put into confuſion, and gave way on all ſides. The Moors being totally ſtrangers in that country, unable to ſecure a retreat, were moſt of them ſlain, as on their account De Gueſclin had adviſed not to give quarter. Amongſt the Caſtilians it was ſingular, that no perſon of rank loſt his life on the ſide of King Peter, except John Ximenes, a knight from Cordova, owing to the ſudden diſorder they were thrown into, many of their out-poſts not having joined them. Martin Lope de Cordova, who was advancing with the rear, perceiving the diſorder of the troops, and that the day was loſt, thought it moſt prudent to retreat, and haſten to Carmona, to protect the King's children, and ſecure the treaſury (U). Even Peter himſelf, finding his army defeated, was obliged, by the advice of Fernando de Caſtro, to take ſhelter in the caſtle of Montiel after this unfortunate encounter, which happened on the 16th of March, 1369, on the memorable plains of Montiel, which ſeparate the kingdom of Caſtile from that of Valencia.

CHAPTER THE TENTH.

King Peter quits the Castle of Montiel, and enters the Tent of De Guesclin.—Is murdered by Henry, who becomes King of Castile.

AS soon as it was known in Henry's army that the King had retreated into the castle of Montiel, orders were given that it should be immediately surrounded with troops, and closely watched, so that nothing could stir out without being instantly perceived. Among the few who got into Montiel with King Peter, there was a knight, whose name was Men Rodriguez de Senabria, who had been taken prisoner at Bribiesca when Henry was first proclaimed king of Castile, and had been ransomed by De Guesclin, on his telling him he was a native of Trastamara, which county was ceded to De Guesclin by Henry. This knight hearing that De Guesclin commanded the detachment that lay before the castle of Montiel, sent a message to let him know he wished for a private conference; which De Guesclin consented to. He then offered him two

two hundred thoufand gold doblas, and many lordfhips and cities in Caftile, if he would fuffer the King to efcape. De Guefclin apprifed Henry of what had paffed, who thanked him, and faid he was better able to give that fum and thofe lordfhips than Peter, and would reward him with them, and engaged him to accept of the conference, and perfuade the King to come to his tent. For this purpofe a fafe-conduct was offered on the oath of De Guefclin and others; but this was no fooner known in the camp, than rumours of treachery were privately circulated. Be that as it may, the unfortunate King, reduced to the laft extremity, fcarce any water left, his army defeated, himfelf deferted by his friends, and the few left unable to affift him, in a fit of defpair finally refolved to go to the tent of De Guefclin. After a few words had paffed, Peter fufpecting his danger faid, "It is time to be gone;" and was going to mount, when he was abruptly told to ftop. Suddenly Henry appeared, armed at all points, and came clofe to King Peter, who did not know him again, not having feen him for a long time; though fome one faid, "Sir, take "care; your enemy is coming." Henry on his part exclaimed, "Where is that Jew who calls "himfelf King of Caftile?" At this the undaunted Peter, rouzed with indignation, inſtantly replied: "Thou art a traitor; I am Peter, "King of Caſtile, lawful ſon of king Alfon-"ſo;" and at the ſame moment grappled with Henry, and being the ſtrongeſt threw him down; then laying his hand on his ſword would certainly have killed him, had not at that moment the viſcount Rocaberti (ſome ſay it was De Gueſclin) ſeized King Peter by the leg, and turning him on one ſide, gave an opportunity to Henry to get uppermoſt; who drawing out a long poignard, plunged it into the boſom of Peter, and, with the aſſiſtance of thoſe preſent, immediately killed him.

Thus, by the hands of his baſtard brother Henry, was miſerably murdered on the 23d of March 1369, in the 36th year of his age, and 19th of his reign, the unfortunate Peter King of Caſtile, the laſt male heir of his line, deſcended from Raymond count of Burgundy, who, about the year 1100, married Urraca, daughter of Alfonſo VI. king of Caſtile.

The body of Peter was left for three days unburied expoſed to the people, out of policy, that

all

The following PEDIGREE of the FAMILY of the HISTORY of the PERSONAGES of th WORK.

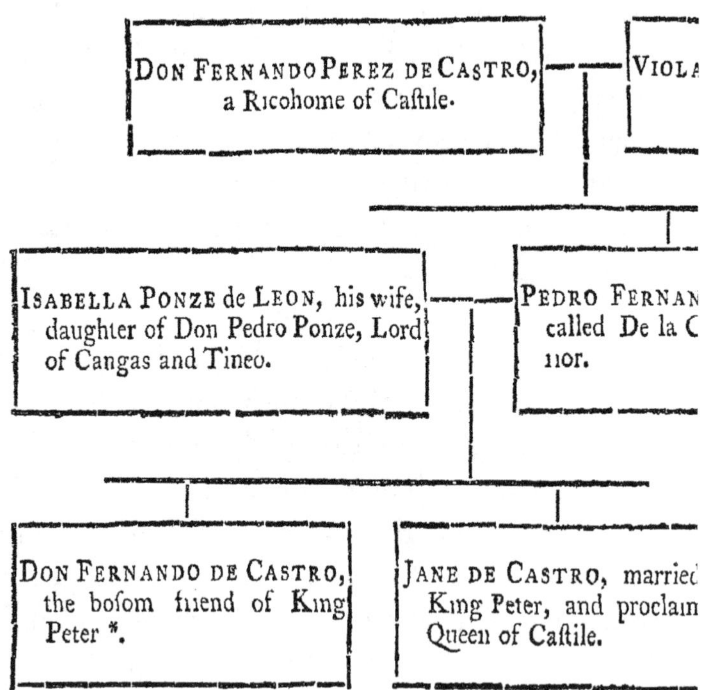

* Don Fernando de Castro, after the death of King Peter, made h he died. Over his tomb was placed the following inscription: A

DE CASTRO, will throw additional light on
hat NAME mentioned in the Course of this

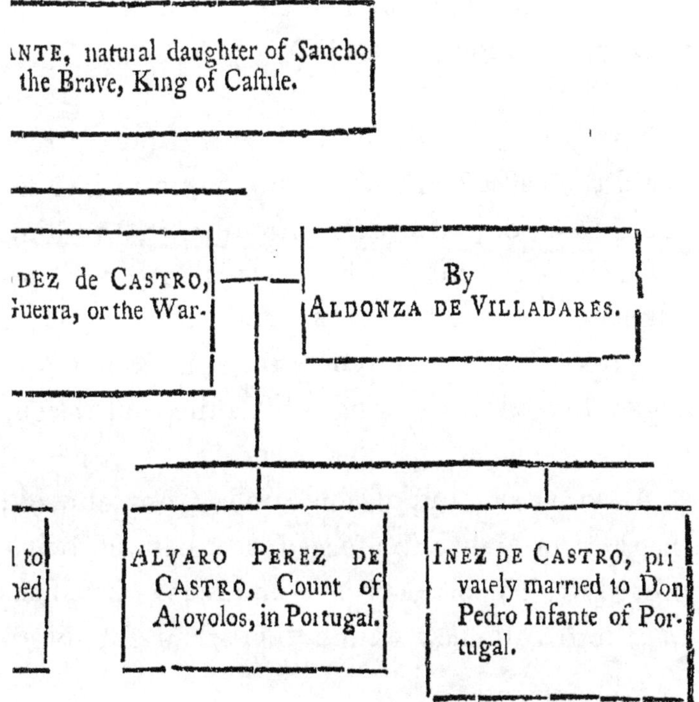

iis escape into Portugal, and afterwards retired to Guyenne, where
QUI YACE DON FERNANDO PEREZ DE CASTRO TODA LA

all ranks might be certain he was no more. With this unfortunate monarch there alſo fell two gallant Engliſhmen, who were ſlain for having drawn their ſwords in his defence when grappling with Henry. Theſe were ſir Ralph Holmes and James Rowland, whoſe ſpirit and bravery deſerved a better fate. The life of Fernando de Caſtro was ſpared on account of his long attachment and fidelity to his ſovereign (W).

THE governor of Montiel immediately ſurrendered the caſtle to Henry, who took him into favour, as he did all others who ſubmitted to him, rewarding generouſly his friends, as well foreigners as his countrymen; and with the TITLE OF HENRY THE SECOND AND THE BOUNTIFUL began his reign as king of Caſtile and Leon,

A VIOLENT oppoſition aroſe from abroad; the right of Henry to ſucceed, as a baſtard, being ſtrongly called in queſtion; and many Caſtilians went into voluntary exile rather than ſubmit to him.

THE king of Portugal claimed the crown of Caſtile, as great-grand-ſon to king Sancho by Beatrix his daughter, and ſent a challenge to Henry. The kings of Navarre and Aragon likewiſe endeavoured to recover thoſe places which they thought they had a right to; but the greateſt ſtorm ſeemed to be from England, where John of Gaunt, duke of Lancaſter, ſtiled himſelf king of Caſtile; and not only demanded that crown in right of Conſtance his wife, daughter to Peter, but embarked for Spain, and headed an army to ſubſtantiate his claim (X).

THE late Peter King of Caſtile was handſome in perſon, and of a fair complexion. He had a ſlight impediment in his ſpeech, and rather ſtammered. What is ſingular, the ſame defect is attributed to his cotemporary Peter king of Portugal. His conſtitution was robuſt, and free from infirmities, enduring all manner of fatigue without the leaſt inconvenience. Like his father, he was fond of the chace, which was the reigning paſſion of the age (Y). He was of an amorous diſpoſition, and extremely inclined to the fair ſex; ſuſpicious, covetous, and ſanguine; valiant withal in the field, in contradiction to the general habits of thoſe vices. Hiſtorians have ſaid that he was a ſtrict diſpenſer of juſtice; that the country was free from robbers during his reign; that evil-

doers

doers ſtood in dread of him, and many quitted the kingdom; for which his countrymen ought to have acknowledged ſome obligation in that ferocious age, when robbery and plunder were ſo common in Europe, and ſcarcely conſidered as offences; particularly in England, where they roſe to ſuch a height, that it was as dangerous to travel there as among the Arabs; inſomuch that Peter king of Cyprus and Jeruſalem, who viſited England about this time, viz. in 1363, had been barbarouſly robbed on the highway, and ſtripped of his money and baggage.

King Peter is generally branded with the epithet of Cruel. Foreign writers ſet no bounds to their acrimony and abuſe. Mattheo Villani, an Italian writer, calls Peter "a cruel and beaſtly king, whoſe royal mind conſiſted of the moſt cruel tyranny; a perverſe intoxicated monarch, the tyrant of Spain, unworthy the name of a king (Z)." Yet after the paſſions of men were cooled, and thoſe were no more, who deprived him of his kingdom, and were intereſted in blackening his fame, he was called *El Juſticiero*. The ſame was alſo obſerved with reſpect to Peter king of Portugal, of whom the Portugueze hiſtorians ſay, that

that he was by ſome called THE CRUEL, by others EXECUTOR OF JUSTICE; which laſt title, they add, more properly belonged to him. The fate of both theſe kings was remarkable: the former was deprived of the realm of Caſtile, and of his life, by his baſtard-brother Henry; and the baſtard ſon of the latter got poſſeſſion of the kingdom of Portugal.

THE

THE ISSUE OF KING PETER.

By MARIA de PADILLA.

BEATRIX; born at Cordova in 1533; became a nun; buried in the royal monastery of St. Clare, in Tordesillas, founded by herself.

CONSTANCE; born at Castro Xeriz, 1354; married to John of Gaunt, duke of Lancaster, who in her right, after the death of King Peter, claimed the crown of Castile.

ISABELLA; born at the village of Morales, near the city of Toro, 1355; married to Edmund Langley, earl of Cambridge, duke of York, by whom he had Richard earl of Cambridge;

bridge; who marrying his coufin Anne Mortimer, heirefs of the Houfe of Clarence, had Richard, duke of York, father of Edward IV. king of England.

Don ALONSO; who died in his infancy.

By the LADY JANE de CASTRO.

DON JOHN; confined as a prifoner in the caftle of Soria, under the care of the alcayde Don Beltran de Eril. He married Elvira, daughter of the alcayde, in hopes of obtaining his enlargement; but this hard-hearted officer, deaf to the intreaties of his daughter, confined his fon-in-law more clofely, and loaded him with irons. He died in prifon of a broken heart. The unfortunate Don John left a fon and a daughter; Peter, bifhop of Ofma; and Conftance, priorefs of the royal convent of St. Dominic in Madrid, where Don John is interred, his corpfe having been conveyed there from the caftle of Soria, by his daughter Conftance, the priorefs, in 1442; by whom an effigy of her unhappy father was fet up with the irons on his legs, and fuitable infcriptions reciting his

wards

birth and misfortunes; but they were afterwards effaced, and his descent called in question.

By a BEDCHAMBER WOMAN of the Court, named ISABELLA, who waited on the Infante DON ALONSO.

DON SANCHO; born at Almazan in 1363; taken prisoner in Carmona after the death of Peter, by Henry the second, and confined in Toledo; and after being removed from fortress to fortress, was finally conducted to Curiel, where he died without issue. His corpse was carried to Toledo, and interred in the church of St. Dominic el Real, in 1448.

DON DIEGO; brother to Don Sancho, taken with him in Carmona; remained fifty-five years a prisoner of state at Curiel, whence he was removed by King John II. to the town of Coca, where he was allowed the liberty of the town, and ended his days there in 1434. By a daughter of the alcayde of Curiel, he left a son and a daughter, Peter and Mary, from whom several noble families claim a descent.

By

By MARIA de AYALA.

MARIA; a nun; prioress of the royal convent of St. Dominic in Toledo; daughter of King Peter, by Teresa de Ayala, daughter of Dia Gomez de Toledo.

KING Peter was buried in Montiel, in a convent of Franciscans built on the occasion, where twelve friars were appointed to pray for his soul. His corpse was removed to the church of St. Jago in La Puebla de Alcocer: and from thence in 1446, by king John II. to the royal convent of St. Dominic in Madrid, where it still remains.

IT appears from this history, that King Peter had three wives at the same time, in opposition to every remonstrance from the head of the church, the representations of his subjects, or the reflections naturally belonging to good example or propriety of conduct. The first wife, according to his own confession and that of his witnesses, was Maria de Padilla. This marriage was private; the next was public and solemn with Blanche of Bourbon in Valladolid; the third was equally public, in the presence of his people, with Jane de Castro, in the town of Cuellar.

QUEEN

QUEEN BLANCHE OF BOURBON is interred in the church of St. Francis, in the city of Xerez de la Frontera in Andalusia, according to the historian Zurita. Long after, an inscription was placed to her memory; tho' the historian Garibay pretends that the French who came into Spain with Trastamara removed her corpse, in order to carry it to France, but were obliged to leave it at Tudela in Navarre: this, however, was a mistake.

MARIA DE PADILLA was first interred in the convent of St. Clare de Estudilla, of her own founding; but when the King declared his marriage to the Cortes, the prelates and nobility were directed to go to Estudilla, and bring her corpse in great pomp to the cathedral of Seville, to be deposited in a vault belonging to the chapel of kings, till a proper chapel could be constructed with becoming splendour, where it was afterwards transferred.

JANE DE CASTRO, proclaimed queen of Castile, is interred in the metropolitan church of St. Jago, where a magnificent tomb was erected to her memory, with the arms and royal crown of Castile, and those of Castro separately with-

without a crown, and the figure of a woman robed in ſtately garments, having a crown on her head. Underneath the following inſcription:

AQUI YACE DONA JUANA DE CASTRO REYNA DE CASTILLA, QUE FINO EN 21 DE AGOSTO, ERA DE 1412.

THE lady Jane de Caſtro was half ſiſter to Ignez de Caſtro, married privately in Portugal to the infante Don Pedro, afterwards king of Portugal. The tragical end of this beautiful lady is related at full length by Faria, in his Hiſtory of Portugal; as well as the cruel death inflicted on her baſe murderers, after they were delivered up by Peter King of Caſtile.

APPEN-

CHAPTER THE ELEVENTH.

Conclufion.—General Obfervations on the Trade and Navigation of Aragon, before and after the Junction of that Crown to the Kingdom of Caftile.—State of the Arts.

HAVING traced the turbulent reign of Peter to its final period, and endeavoured to exhibit a candid picture of the manners and cuftoms of that ferocious age, I have thought that fome further reflections on the trade and navigation of both kingdoms, particularly the wife regulations of the Aragonefe, might tend to give inlight to the hiftory of that period, and ferve as a further illuftration of the political and maritime ftate of both kingdoms in the fourteenth and fifteenth centuries; inafmuch as they will be explanatory in fome degree of that jealoufy and animofity which fubfifted between the two kingdoms, and occafioned the fitting out fuch confiderable armaments in the Mediterranean as have been mentioned in the courfe of this Hiftory. At the fame time I acknowledge my obligations for this information to that ingenious and learned academician Don Antonio de Campmani y de Montpaleu, whoſe curious memoirs on the antient commerce of Barcelona, I have already had occaſion to ſpeak of, with that applauſe due to his learned reſearches.

THE principal mart of the commerce of Aragon was undoubtedly the city of Barcelona, governed by a council of worthy citizens and traders, intereſted in the welfare of commerce and navigation, and verſed by practical knowledge and experience in its different branches.

THIS council conſiſted of two hundred members, all reſpectable men in different profeſſions, acquainted with every part of political and mercantile adminiſtration; whoſe repreſentations were laid before the ſovereign, and attended to with the utmoſt deference, as will appear from the different grants and privileges enacted in favour of trade by king James I. and Peter III. of Aragon, at the particular deſire of magiſtracy, for the general good and advantage of the ſtate; which ordinances were ſo prudent and wiſe, that foreign nations imitated them, and introduced ſimilar regulations.

To these sage magistrates the province of Catalonia is indebted for many privileges in favour of arts, manufactures, and commerce; the establishment of foreign consuls; regulations for insurances, exchanges, brokers, and divers matters of an inferior nature, for the general good of trade and navigation, as well to prevent wars with their neighbours, as to establish new treaties of peace on the most advantageous and favourable terms.

The first record from whence the spirit of commerce in those seas may be adduced, according to the learned writer before-mentioned, will be found so early as 1068, in the law *omnes quippe naves*; wherein Raymond the second, Count of Barcelona, grants protection to all vessels that frequent the ports of his dominions. These hospitable laws were confirmed at the Cortes of Barcelona, in 1283, by king Peter III. also by king Alonso III. at the Cortes of Monzon in 1289; and, finally, by king James II. in the Cortes of Barcelona, in 1299.

These princes not only attended to the increase of the trade of their subjects, but encouraged them on the principles observed in modern times; giving every preference to the ſhips of their own ſubjects, in excluſion of foreign veſſels.

KING James I. was ſo ſtrenuous in this particular, from a ſenſe of its importance in favour of his naval power, that in the year 1227 he enacted a law in favour of the city of Barcelona, ſtating that no foreign ſhip ſhould load for Syria or Alexandria, while a ſhip belonging to that city could be found in their port able to perform the voyage. By another *Cedula*, or grant, of the year 1230, a free trade was allowed with the iſlands of Majorca and Iviza, by ſea and land, exempt from all duties and cuſtoms whatever. By another of 1232, the citizens of Barcelona were exempt from all duties of tranſit or exciſe; and to enjoy a perfect freedom in their perſons, ſervants, and merchandize, throughout the dominion of the crown of Aragon, by ſea and land. This was again confirmed by Peter IV. in 1343; and in conſequence, the citizens of Barcelona furniſhed ample ſupplies of money and ſhipping for the expedition againſt the iſland of Majorca.

THE different ports of Catalonia being ſubject in thoſe days to a variety of contributions impoſed by different lords of manors, who levied ſums from

from the ſhipping, under the claim of territorial juriſdiction, to the great annoyance of trade; king James I. as a further encouragement to navigation, freed the ſhips of Barcelona in 1265, from all impoſt dues to the abbot of San Felis de Guixols, hitherto claimed on the entrance, or ſailing from that harbour. Further, in 1282, at the requeſt of the magiſtracy, the two per cent. port dues of the harbour of Blanes were aboliſhed, and declared to be unjuſt, and prejudicial to commerce.

He further, in 1265, to promote trade among his own ſubjects, ordered all the merchants from Florence, Sienna, Lucca, with the Lombards, to depart from Barcelona, and never more be permitted to have warehouſes and ſhops in that city. Further, no foreigner, either mariner or tradeſman, was to keep a ſhop, or ſhip goods not belonging to themſelves in any other veſſel but thoſe belonging to his kingdom.

The city of Barcelona, finding great prejudice to their navigation from a duty on exportation laid by the ſovereign on ſundry goods, on repreſenting the ſame to king Peter III. he repealed it in 1218, granting them licence freely to export all manner of goods beyond ſea, wheat and barley excepted, unlefs the quantity at market admitted of it. The fame with refpect to cordage, arms, and utenfils, for infidel ftates; with a referve for horfes that might be fent to Paleftine for the ufe of the croifaders.

Every day brought forward new grants and favours in behalf of trade and navigation. A new act of king Peter III. breathes the true fpirit of commercial freedom. (See *Couftitude Catal.* lib. iv. tit. xxv. page 299.) By the 13th chapter, merchant adventurers and feamen are not to be ftopped from proceeding on their voyages, by any judicial arreft, once their veffel is launched or ready to be launched, provided they give fecurity to anfwer in court at their return. All new dues were to be abolifhed that had been impofed in the ports of Barcelona, Corvera, Llanza, Palamos, Montblanc, Tamaril, Tortofa, and other places, on the fhips from Andalufia or more diftant feas. All veffels fitted out by the magiftrates of Barcelona were exempt from all dues on failing from, or to, any port of their dominion. Veffels coming to an anchor in any port or road, that do not unload, are not to pay any fees whatever.

For

As a further encouragement to the fisheries, King Peter III. took off all duties and customs on salt, at the Cortes of Barcelona, in 1283, engaging for himself and his successors that they should never be renewed: this was particularly advantageous to the Tunny-fishery, which was considerable on that coast.

The fees on shipwrecks had been abolished in ancient times, but still abuses had crept in; for which reason king Alonso III. in 1286, issued express and peremptory orders, that no person should receive any fees for shipwrecks or vessels stranded on any part of his coasts; and further enacted a liberty of buying and selling freely all manner of goods and wares without any duty whatever, naval stores excepted, and corn when royal fleets were fitting out. But in peaceable times these articles were free to be exported every where, except to the Infidels.

In the Cortes of Barcelona, in 1299, by the 10th article, king James II. annulled all duties on the exportation of corn, provisions, and other articles, either for Christians or Infidels, with an exception to the enemies of the Crown, and a reserve for corn and products of the land in times of scarcity.

To obviate the frequent use of letters of marque, so prejudicial to commerce, between the crowns of France and Aragon, at the beginning of the 14th century, it was agreed, in 1313, between Philip de Valois and James II. of Aragon, that in future no letters of marque should be granted, under pretence of retaliation; unless it could be proved that nine months had elapsed after the requisition, without satisfaction given to the petitioning party. It was further settled that, in case of absence of the sovereign, a competent tribunal should be appointed reciprocally; that is, in Paris, before commissioners named for the purpose; or in Barcelona, before the procurator-general or his deputy, that the complaint may be established, and a proof of refusal of justice, before any letters of marque should be granted on either side. If this was not observed, the king was to pay all damages occurred, when the embargo was taken off.

The custom of fitting out privateers had been so universal that, even after peace was declared, they continued sending out ships, and committing divers acts of piracy; insomuch that the Catalonians, Majorquins, Genoese, and Saoenese were

were a nuiſance to the coaſt of France, and the commerce of Languedoc; which occaſioned a variety of applications to Philip de Valois, who annulled all the vexations of his maritime ſubjects. James II. renewed all the penalties againſt the Lombards, as well as againſt the Florentines and other Italian ſtates, prohibiting them to dwell in Barcelona, or to carry on any trade there, either directly or indirectly, under very ſevere penalties. However, ſome merchants of Piſa were permitted to trade, on petition to Peter III. and were received by a particular licence as friends and allies.

In 1356, on account of the war with Genoa, King Peter gave leave to trade in foreign bottoms to all countries in amity with his kingdom, provided they did not ſend away his own ſubjects.

To protect the property of the merchants of Barcelona, who had been plundered by privateers from Piſa, king Martin gave orders, in 1397, to Pedro Queralt, who was going to Italy with two gallies, to ſeize upon all the veſſels of Piſa, till he had ſatisfaction for the damages complained of. The Italians became ſo troubleſome to the trade of his ſubjects, by divers frauds and mal-

practices,

practices, that he found himself obliged, by a public decree, in 1401, to expel them out of his dominions with all their effects; not even permitting them to trade in their own name or in partnership; and only permitted them to enter the kingdom with a safe-conduct, when coming with corn in times of scarcity.

The citizens of Genoa and Pisa, as well as the Tuscans and Florentines, already married and settled in the country, or the sons of such, born in the state of Catalonia, were not included in this prohibition, provided they did not act as agents for those included in the penalties abovementioned.

The trade of Barcelona had now arrived to such a flourishing state, that they compiled a general Book of Rates under Ferdinand IV. in 1413, of all the duties on exportation and imports in use at that period.

By the first article, all goods imported or exported, paid a duty of two-thirds per cent. on the value of the purchase, except the goods from Turkey, Syria, and Egypt, which paid one-third per cent. on the value on importation.

By the fourth article, grain, vegetables, wine and pork, were imported duty free; but five per cent. on exportation, except for the islands of Majorca, Minorca, and Iviza.

By the fourteenth article, all plate, jewels, arms, wearing-apparel, and trinkets, if imported as articles of trade, paid two and a half per cent.

By the sixteenth, all goods which arrived at any port that were not landed or reshipped, paid no duty.

By the eighteenth, all cloth or other manufactures exported to foreign markets, or imported for fairs at home, went duty free, except at the place of sale, when they only paid three quarters per cent.; and half that sum, if manufactures of the province.

By the twentieth, all ships built in the province for sale abroad, with all timber for ship-building, paid three per cent. on exportation, except masts and yards, and other spare timber and materials for the ship's use in case of accident at sea.

By the twentieth, all goods, whose value did not exceed five sueldos, (about one pound five shillings), paid no duty either in or out.

By

By the twenty-first, all articles exported and that were to return again, such as casks, barrels, wrappers, and such like, were duty free.

It was difficult to decide which regulations were most salutary and favourable to commerce; whether those of the crown, or of the court of citizens. The most ancient municipal regulation bears date in 1238, for the regulation of ships in the merchants service; and is, perhaps, the most ancient code of mercantile statutes in Europe. It contains twenty articles for the government of masters of ships, mates, pilots, clerks, mariners, and factors; freights of goods, anchorage, loading and unloading; the duties of each individual reciprocally, and every thing essential respecting navigation, with the conduct of mariners in the merchants service.

To give further energy to their national acts of navigation, a new municipal order was issued, that no goods could be shipped in the port of Barcelona, but on vessels belonging to the king's subjects; with an additional ordinance, in 1436, respecting the payment of seamen's wages, their obedience to the masters of vessels, and penalties on refusing to pursue their voyages, or absenting themselves from

from the ſhips. On the other hand, the maſters were bound to deliver their accounts to the owners, on the return of each voyage; all which were to be ſettled by the proper parties, before the ſhip proceeded on a new voyage. In a word, the wiſeſt and moſt wholeſome regulations between the merchant and mariner, for the mutual benefit of both parties, were laid down, with a preciſion and equity that would do honour to the moſt enlightened ages or kingdoms.

Nor ſhould I omit mentioning the early date, as well as the wiſdom and policy, of the ſtates of Barcelona with reſpect to inſurances of ſhips, one of the greateſt benefits to a commercial nation; and which has ariſen to ſo high a pitch of credit and reputation in England. The code of laws of Barcelona reſpecting this important branch of commerce, is very advantageous to the merchant; and the inhabitants of Catalonia may, perhaps, boaſt of being the earlieſt, as well as the beſt informed, and moſt judicious adventurers.

Notwithstanding the advantages they received from their act of navigation in favour of their maritime commerce, there were not wanting enemies of their ſucceſs, who ſpirited

the

the people to remonſtrate againſt the ſuppoſed injuſtice of thoſe laws, and the excluſion of foreigners, and excited their friends to petition for an alteration; but king Alonſo and his council were too wiſe to give credit to ſuch clamour; and the acts of navigation were confirmed, and as far as neceſſary rendered more effective.

Most of theſe regulations, founded on the ſecureſt baſis of national intereſt and proſperity, loſt in ſome degree their full effect from a variety of cauſes, after the junction of the crown of Aragon to that of Caſtile. Whether from jealouſy, different diſpoſitions, local circumſtances or cuſtoms, or whatever elſe may have been the cauſe, the ſame laws, which ſeem ſo well calculated for the advantage of one kingdom, met with obſtacles when communicated to the other; and much ſtrife and bickerings aroſe in this conteſt. The ſageſt laws were miſrepreſented, or improperly applied, to colour partial views and intereſts; which formed ſuch a chaos of reaſoning and politics, as blended the ſimpleſt facts with the moſt abſtruſe argument, and interwove truth and fable ſo artfully together, as to perplex the ſincereſt endeavours of the candid and moſt liberal; ſo that during the reigns of the Auſtrian

Auftrian princes, the two kingdoms feemed to have feparate interefts, and endeavouring to take advantage of each other. Each kingdom was taken up with impofitions of new duties and cuftoms, which heightened animofity, eftranged the two kingdoms from each other, and made them appear as jealous rivals and fecret enemies, rather than friends and brethren. This overbearing and unhofpitable fpirit of the Caftilians was oppofed by an act for the encouragement of navigation, (held by the emperor Charles V. at Barcelona, in 1520) wherein it was ordained, that no veffel not belonging to the king's fubjects, could load falt, wool, grain, or fruit, in the ports of Spain, with a preference to the Aragonefe over the Caftilians, from the port of Carthagena eaftward, in counterpoife to the preference which the Caftilians had previoufly obtained in their favour in all their own ports. At the fame time the Aragonefe ftrongly inveighed againft this partiality of the Caftilians, who would not admit the Catalonians to participate with them in the freedom of their ports, hardly confidering them as free-born fubjects, entitled to a generous communication of thofe privileges which they expected as a fifter kingdom, who gave them every proof of fincere attachment, ferved them in their wars, and heartily

tily joined iſſue in their proſperity and glory. Theſe benefits were reſerved for the reign of the Bourbon family, when the principles of univerſal commerce being better underſtood, the Aragoneſe were admitted to thoſe rights which they were entitled to expect as men and brethren, united by every tie of intereſt and affection in the common cauſe of the Spaniſh monarchy, and its happineſs and ſplendour, on the broad ſcale of univerſal equity and juſtice, by which mankind are bound together by the ſolemn ties of reciprocal amity, protection, and intereſt.

Having ſaid ſo much reſpecting the laws of navigation, it ſeems incumbent to add a few words reſpecting the arts, and their progreſs and eſtimation in foreign countries, in conſequence of the laws enacted for their encreaſe and ſupport. By this comparative view we ſhall be able to form one grand commercial outline, and ſhew the notions and principles of trade in the Mediterranean; and the proportion in which they ſtood in that age, in point of ability, genius, and mercantile ſpirit with England; which, by its conſtant attention to thoſe objects, has riſen to that magnitude and power, in which all the world beholds it with admiration and ſurprize.

THE trade of the Catalonians has been ſhewn to be not merely paſſive; on the contrary, a moſt active commerce, in which the products of the country, with their ſuperfluities, were exported in their own bottoms, foſtered by every encouragement that different acts of navigation could afford them; further cheriſhed by frugality, a plentiful country, and an induſtrious and laborious diſpoſition: to crown all, their magiſtrates were traders united in ſocial ties to fit out large and ſtout ſhips proper for long voyages, where conſiderable expences were required.

AMONG many articles of their export trade, their woollen manufactures ſtood in the firſt claſs, as well as thoſe of cotton, in which the town of Mancheſter has at preſent rendered its fame ſo univerſal in every part of the globe. In thoſe days the manufacturers of Catalonia were no leſs diſtinguiſhed; the works of their ingenious artiſts were in the higheſt eſtimation in Italy, Egypt, Syria, and every part of the Levant, excluſive of the demand in the Italian ſtates, Sicily, and Sardinia; which, almoſt down to the preſent age, have continued their attachment to thoſe articles.

The woollen cloths of Barcelona were in high esteem in Seville in King Peter's reign, and in the preceding century. So far back as 1243, the woollen cloth of Lerida is spoken of in terms of great estimation. A few years after, the towns of Banolas, Valis, Gerona, Perpignan, and Tortosa, were remarkable as manufacturing towns, and for the fineness of their cloths, fustians, and serges. So great was their exportation that, in 1353, on board of a ship from Barcelona, bound to Alexandria, taken by a privateer of Genoa, at the entrance of the Archipelago, among other articles they found her cargo to consist of nine hundred and thirty-five bales of cloth of different colours. And in 1412, Antonio Doria, in the port of Callus, captured three Catalonian ships, on board of which were found near one thousand bales of cloth, besides many other valuable articles.

It further appears upon record, that these ingenious manufacturers not only carried on a considerable trade in the articles of their own immediate fabrics, but were very industrious in imitating the woollen cloths of England, the serges of Ireland, the camblets of Rheims, and the other light stuffs of Flanders; of all which there are many evident proofs in the history of the

times;

times; of which the ingenious author, from whom I borrow theſe remarks, has deduced the moſt ample and indiſputable authority. That their cloths were in great eſteem in France, will appear from the complaints of the merchants of Languedoc, at a time when the French manufactories were abſolutely prohibited in Catalonia.

But what will ſeem in a manner a paradox, in a country of ſuch mercantile activity, is, that great quantities of raw materials were equally exported; and that large parcels of wool were ſent by the river Ebro to Italy, particularly to Lombardy; where, in the fifteenth century, there were eleven cities noted for their woollen manufactures, which wrought nine thouſand pieces of cloth per annum, according to Marino Sanuto, a cotemporary author. (*Vite di Duchi de Venezia apud Muratori, tom.* xxii. *page* 952.) who further inſiſts that the Catalonians exported annually, to Lombardy, wool to the value of one hundred and twenty thouſand Venetian ducats. At the ſame time theſe wiſe traders prohibited the importation of all ſorts of foreign cloth, ſilk, gold or ſilver tiſſues, &c. in order to oblige their countrymen to make uſe of and encourage their own manufactures Not only their artiſts had riſen to ſuch a perfection for their own manufactures, but even those of other countries received from them a new dye or polish, and were again re-exported.

Of these facts the proceedings of the Cortes give ample testimony; and their records specify many circumstances in corroboration thereof; where it appears that the merchants, manufacturers, dyers, and artists, were particularly consulted, not to enter into useless speculations on the political interests of the state, but merely respecting the perfection of various branches of their art, the modes of correcting inconveniencies, and meliorating particular parts, of which they were competent judges; such, for example, as the method of dyeing, and employing madder, kermes, and other ingredients.

The fustian weavers were known so far back as 1253. The manufacturers of cotton were the next in consequence, as well as the spinning thereof; for the encouragement of which, a duty of fifty per cent. was laid upon foreign cotton and yarn imported. The same duty was also laid on foreign manufacture. In 1481 their own manufactures had risen to great perfection, such as all kinds of vessels of tin, copper, iron, steel, also leather, and

and wearing apparel; but with refpect to the filk manufactures, they were far exceeded by the kingdom of Granada, poffeffed by the Moors, who had received thofe ingenious arts from the Arabians, and had likewife introduced them into Andalufia. The filk manufacture alfo formed a valuable branch of commerce of the Caftilians with the Catalonians, who, by means of the port of Almeria, imported thofe articles largely for the ornament of churches, and the fplendid drefs of the nobility on feftivals and at tournaments, which were in great vogue in the fourteenth century.

Were I to enter into details of the products of the foil, and to fpeak of their exports of oil, honey, wines, faffron, and fruits, it would require a more minute inveftigation than the nature of the prefent difquifition will admit of. Some parts of thefe products I have already expatiated upon in my Travels through Spain, principally intended as an effay towards the natural hiftory of that kingdom; though I acknowledge that much remains ftill to be added on that fubject, in a kingdom fo fertile and abundant.

Among many other articles of foreign commerce, the building of fhips feems not to have been the leaſt conſiderable ; but it is probable, that when once a ſhip was ſold to a foreign merchant, who had fairly paid for the ſame, it became the abſolute property of that ſtate to which the merchant belonged, when navigated according to law, and was authorized to export every article of commerce.

We are now to add a few words reſpecting the citizens, with the riſe of the mechanic arts, and the labours of the general claſs of inhabitants, whoſe induſtry laid the foundation of opulence to their deſcendants, and raiſed them to a more eligible ſtate of independence than was to be acquired by the profeſſion of arms, and thoſe hazardous enterprizes which had no other baſis than romantic honour, and the trifling conſequence of perſonal valour and heroic enthuſiaſm.

While the maritime province of Barcelona remained ſubject to the Lords aſſembled in the Cortes, who formed an ariſtocracy, there was little to be expected from the people, where the feudal ſyſtem granted no favours, and on whom the Lords looked down with a contemptuous frown; but no ſooner were the Commons

mons enabled to emerge from this obſcurity, and obtain a charter from Peter the Fourth, permitting them to ſit as repreſentatives in the Cortes for the cities and towns, than the voice of liberty animated their efforts, and made their conſequence conſpicuous. The ſovereigns were glad to raiſe up theſe frugal men as a barrier againſt the haughtineſs and pride of the Barons. The citizens formed themſelves into guilds and trading ſocieties, increaſed their affluence, became magiſtrates, made laws for the government of their fellow-citizens, put arms into their hands, coined money, and ſhewed themſelves worthy of the higheſt truſt; and by the love of their country, moral characters, and decent deportment, eclipſed the tranſient luſtre of the nobles, and were admired by the people as the principal ſages in whom they placed confidence and truſt. The Commons, at the ſame time, looking up to the ſovereign whom they conſidered as their protector, who freed them from the oppreſſion of the Lords, and the hardſhips of the feudal ſyſtem, were liberal in their aids to the crown, and forward in their grants of monies and ſhips. The cities were rebuilt, and population increaſed, while the jealous Barons remained immured in their gloomy

 caſtles,

caſtles, following the beaſts of the field, and filling their minds with the vain atchievements of the Cruſaders, the deluſive paſſion of arms, and the falſe glory of conqueſt.

If we contemplate the induſtry of the cities, peace and harmony increaſed their numbers and fortunes, liberty encouraged their labours, and ſecured the fruits of their toil. The arts, undiſturbed by invidious diſtinctions, roſe every day to a higher perfection.

To evince the true ſpirit of mercantile liberty unſhackled by thoſe mean and narrow-minded limitations of the northern guilds, every encouragement was given to the ſettlement of induſtrious foreigners. Inſtead of confining the privileges of a citizen to the natives of Barcelona, James the Second extended it to every one of his ſubjects who had a ſettlement there. Theſe laws took place ſo early as the year 1306, in favour of ſuch as had reſided there for a year and a day. From theſe aroſe the early appearance of aſſociated companies of mechanics and tradeſmen in different branches, as far back as 1208. The benefice of St. Mark, in the Cathedral of Barcelona, was founded by the company of ſhoemakers. The

guilds

guilds of armourers, arrowſmiths, ſword-cutlers, and others, were all known in the thirteenth century, and ſupplied the Venetians, the Caſtilians, and other ſtates. The demand for arms was ſo great, that in 1388 John the firſt King of Caſtile, ſon of the baſtard Henry, applied to the magiſtrates of Barcelona for a thouſand cheſts of arrows to carry on the war againſt Portugal. The armoury of that city was famous in Europe in thoſe days: King Alfonſo uſed to term it The Trojan Horſe of his kingdom. Even the ſtreets of the city bore the names of upwards of five-and-twenty mechanic arts, which were common there; ſome of which occupied the whole ſtreet. In a word, the city reſembled a bee-hive, where every mechanic art was encouraged and followed with indefatigable induſtry. The citizens were united to each other by every tie that endears ſociety, diveſted of invidious diſtinctions. Every claſs of mechanics being found equally enlightened and zealous in the common cauſe, none were excepted, not even butchers, from participating of thoſe rights which belonged to them as men in ſocial concord, inſpired with the nobleſt paſſion in the human breaſt, a love for their country.

In speaking of the state of the arts, manufactures, and navigation of those days, it is singular to observe the early attempts towards commercial liberty, and the subsequent fetters thrown on trade by a monopolizing spirit, and a selfishness that vainly thought to let no other nation partake of it, and engross all the trade of the world to themselves. By a statute of the 25th of Edward III. cap. 3. that of the ninth of that king was confirmed in favour of foreign merchants; granting licence to all persons, as well foreigners as natives, to buy and sell by wholesale and retail, where, when, and how they pleased, paying the usual duties and customs, notwithstanding any grant or usages to the contrary; seeing such usages and grants are to the common prejudice of the king and his people. But this excellent and well-judged act was not permitted to remain in force; which prevented the commercial increase of the nation. The monopolizing grants of the crown that followed in subsequent reigns, with the narrow spirit of corporations, checked the ardour of individuals, and caused evils which the liberal and generous foreign merchant endeavoured in vain to counteract.

A singular contrast further appears on comparing the naval power of England and Spain in those

those days. The Spaniards had larger vessels than ours, and for a time seemed to give laws in our Channel; insomuch that Edward the Third issued his mandates to the clergy, "to put up "prayers, make processions, say masses, and distri- "bute alms, for imploring the divine clemency, "and the appeasing God's anger:" that the Spaniards had not only taken and destroyed many English vessels laden with wines, but threatened no less than the destruction of the English navy; boasting withal their intention to reign masters of the English seas, and even to invade the kingdom of England and subdue the people; which occasioned a duty of forty-pence per ton to be laid on all wines coming from Bourdeaux, for guarding the seas against the Spaniards. The king further sent a mandate to the magistrates of Bayonne, reciting the formidable power of the Spaniards, and ordering them to make war on their ships wherever they should meet with them. The event of this injunction has been already recited, our archers proving superior to the Spanish cross-bowmen; and in consequence of the signal victory obtained, King Peter was glad to make a truce with England for twenty years.

NOT-

NOTWITHSTANDING the many cruelties complained of in these naval depredations of the Spaniards, their humane laws relating to ship-wreck, and the usage to be shewn on such unfortunate occasions, breathe a spirit of civilization and compassion, in contradiction to the ferocity of the naval commanders, which seemed to characterize a barbarous disposition. An ordonnance of Alfonso III. which I have already alluded to in this chapter, will elucidate this fact *.

(A. D 1286.)

* Noverint universi, quod cum nobis Alfonso, Dei gratia regi Aragonum Majoricarum et Valentiæ ac comiti Barchinonæ extiterit significatum, quod quidam de Cathalonia præsumpserunt extorquere in aliquibus locis Cathaloniæ sub prætextu naufragii quasdam res, quæ de quibusdam barchis et lignis periclitatis fuerant salvæ factæ et hoc sit contra jus et justitiam; idcirco constituimus et ordinamus ex certa scientia, quod de cætero in tota Cathalonia non audeat aliquis, cujuscumque conditionis existat, capere vel usurpare, aut etiam detinere aliquas res nomine naufragii, vel etiam trobaduræ quæ fuerint de aliquibus navibus, lignis barchis, vel aliis vasis periclitatis, aut periclitantibus. Mandantes Vicariis, Bajulis, et aliis omnibus officialibus et subditis nostris Cathaloniæ præsentibus et futuris, quod hanc nostram ordinationem et mandatum observent et ab omnibus faciant inviolabiter observari. Et si forte inve-

It ſeems very extraordinary, that while ſuch laws were enacted, the moſt barbarous habits exiſted amongſt mariners of diſtinguiſhed characters; and that even the refined Republics of Italy, which boaſted of their ſuperiority over the northern nations, exhibited a cruel temper at ſea when the fortune of war threw the enemy into their power. The Venetian admiral André Dandolo was ſo ſenſible of this, that when he was obliged (in 1292) to ſurrender with a fleet of 65 gallies to Lampa Doria, of Geneva, he ſtruck his head with violence againſt the mainmaſt, which occaſioned his death, to avoid a more cruel fate from the enemy. If this event did not happen, the moſt ſcurrilous and indecent language took place on both ſides. The Venetians having heard that a Genoeſe admiral had ſaid, "Let us go "and deſtroy that herd of ſwine," they ſent out a ſquadron to revenge the inſult; the reſpective

invenerint aliquos qui contra prædictam ordinationem mandatum noſtrum venire præſumpſerint, volumus et mandamus eis, quod ab ipſis pœna legitima ſine omni remedio puniantur. Datum Barchinonæ, quarto Kal. Aprilis anno domini milleſimo ducenoteſſimo octogeſimo ſexto.

Sig+num Alfonſi Dei gratia reg's Aragonum, Majoricanum et Valentiæ ac comitis Barchinonæ.

In Lib Virido, fol. 74, A. M. B.

ad-

admirals hailing each other conſtantly with the opprobrious epithets of Dogs, Swine, and others ſtill more injurious, and, when the opportunity offered, ſpilling the blood of their enemies as freely as that of wild beaſts.

It has been reported, that a ſimilar vivacity of language has ſometimes fallen to the ſhare of modern admirals: that one ſaid of the other, ſwearing moſt vehemently, in conſequence of a ſuppoſition of his having broken his parole of honour, that if "ever he could take him, he would "chain him down to the quarter-deck like a mon-"key:" and that this being reported to the other party, he replied, "If ever he falls to my lot, I "will put him into a cage, and carry him about the "country, to ſhew him at fairs like a ſavage." But theſe are exuberances, unworthy to be dwelt on in ſpeaking of ſuch reſpectable characters; and are only glanced at, as merely deſcriptive, in a philoſophic diſquiſition of the paſſions of mankind, independent of numberleſs inſtances which may be adduced of the nobleſt feelings and generous actions from a ſet of men the glory of their country, and who have paſſed the greater part of their lives on the waves.

I FLAT-

I FLATTER myſelf that this ſtate of the Mediterranean trade may not be unacceptable, but tend to relieve the mind from thoſe ſcenes of bloodſhed which not only ſtamped the character of the King of Caſtile, but were in general the defects of the age. They may ſerve as a contraſt when compared to modern times, in this happy country in particular, where Benevolence forms a leading feature, and where Liberty ſeems to have planted its ſtandard, and Commerce fixed its emporium with ſuch vigour, as, I hope, bids fair to remain unrivalled to the lateſt period of time.

NOTES

APPENDIX,

CONTAINING

NOTES and ILLUSTRATIONS.

(NOTE A, Page 3.)

IF the King had been ſuch a ſavage monſter and tyrant as his enemies repreſented, it would ſeem impoſſible for ſuch a prince to have aſſembled an army at any rate; but it appears beyond contradiction, that many noble lords ſupported him to the laſt, and defended the towns with infinite bravery and perſeverance. Excluſive of thoſe mercenary levies known by the name of Companions, ſtanding armies were unknown at that period: the only method of raiſing troops at that juncture in Caſtile, was by the ſovereign applying to the Infantes and *Ricos Hombres*, engaging them by donatives to ſummons their vaſſals, bring them into the field in defence of the lord paramount: ſome of thoſe *Ricos Hombres* brought two and three hundred retainers along with them. This mode had continued from the invaſion of the Moors till the reign of king John I. in 1446; who finding that theſe lords, uniting with the knights of the military orders, gave riſe to endleſs factions and diſturbances in the kingdom, the antient method of levies was annulled; more regular armies were eſtabliſhed, the offices of conſtable, marſhal, and captains inſtituted, and the old ſyſtem fell into oblivion. The captains were placed in lieu of thoſe turbulent lords ſtiled *Infanzones*, who were ſtill troubleſome in Biſcay and Guypuſcoa, till Henry IV. demoliſhed many of their caſtles about the year 1457, and pacified his kingdom.

Though the kings of Caſtile new-modelled their armies, a long time paſſed before their authority acquired that ſplendour obſerved in modern times. The Caſtilians even boaſt of that ſimplicity of character which made them reſpect their ſovereigns, without the addition of thoſe flattering titles, and complimentary additions, which they learned from their connections with the Italian ſtates. The only title they gave their kings

kings was Grace, or at moſt Lordſhip; which pleaſed them better than the appellation of Highneſs, and Serene Highneſs, given to Ferdinand and Iſabel after the conqueſt of the new world. Finally, the Emperor Charles V. was ſaluted with Majeſty, and Sacred Majeſty, as head of the ſacred Roman empire;—which titles were continued to his poſterity.

In Aragon, where every refinement ſeems of an earlier date than in Caſtile, the title of Majeſty had made an earlier appearance; for in the chronicle of Pedro Lope de Ayala, Queen Eleanor gave the title of Majeſty to King Peter her nephew, according to the cuſtom of Aragon, though the ſame writer never uſes it in ſpeaking of his own country.

(Note B, Page 6.)

THE reſiſtance of the inhabitants of Calagurris, when beſieged by the Romans, forms a remarkable ſtory in the annals of that period, mentioned by Valerius Maximus, who relates, that rather than yield when periſhing with hunger, they preferred devouring their wives and children; and held out till the place was taken by ftorm, and they were all put to the fword; fo that *fames Calagurris* became ever after a proverbial expreffion among the Romans. The emperor Auguftus was fo ftruck with this example of attachment, that, when he returned to Rome, he chofe to have a body-guard compofed of fuch refolute men.

(Note C, Page 10.)

THE magnificent convent of Bernardine nuns, near the city of Burgos, called *Neuftra Senora de Las Huelgas*, with the royal hofpital annexed to it, was founded by Alonfo VIII. king of Caftile, who is interred there, with the princefs Eleanor of England his queen, daughter of our Henry II.

This edifice is truly fplendid and royal. The lady abbefs enjoys many extraordinary privileges, fuperior to any other foundation in Spain. She ftiles herfelf, "By the grace of God and the holy apoftolic fee, lady abbefs of the royal monaftery of Las Huelgas, of the order of St. Bernard, near the city of Burgos; fuperiorefs, matron, prelate, and legal adminiftratrix of the fame, in fpirituals

and

and temporals; and of all the churches, convents, hermitages, and pariſhes belonging to its juriſdiction; by virtue of apoſtolic bulls; with powers, *omni modo privativa quaſi epiſcopalis nullius dioceſis*, exerciſed by royal authority and licence, with public notoriety." This dignified lady further iſſues *demiſſoria* for holy orders, licenſes preachers, and publiſhes cenſures in her eccleſiaſtical courts, with other prerogatives and immunities unknown to her ſex, (ſome of the ſovereign principalities of Germany excepted) which decorate in a high degree her exalted character; her authority extending over thirteen towns and about fifty villages, where ſhe appoints prelates and magiſtrates.

The hoſpital contains commodious apartments for her officers, who are dignified clergy of the religious and military order of Calatrava, with a confeſſor, who is generally a foreigner, to afford comfort to the pilgrims who reſort to the ſhrine of St. James of Compoſtella in Galicia.

Alfonso XI. was crowned here; and a remarkable inſtance reſpecting royalty attended that ceremony: for the intrepid king having ordered the crown to be placed on the altar, he took it with his own hand, and placed it on his head, in presence of the archbishop of St. Jago, who stood by him; the monarch little thinking, after so bold an action, that it would so soon fall from the brows of his son Peter.

(Note D, Page 11.)

DE GUESCLIN having been taken prisoner at the battle of Nagera, lost immediately the counties of Trastamara, Lemos, and Saria, bestowed on him by Henry To repair this disappointment, he now conferred on him the considerable lordships of Molina and Soria, with the title of duke thereof: but these possessions did not seem very accepttable to him; for he afterwards sold them to Henry for one hundred and fifty thousand doblas, and returned to France.

(Note E, Page 11.)

THE count of Denia, marquis of Villena, of the house of Aragon, the steady friend of Henry of Trastamara, was taken prisoner at the battle

battle of Nagera, by two English esquires in the retinue of sir John Chandos, viz. Robert Hawley and John Shekel; the story of which may be found at full length in our historians, relating the ill consequences ensuing, and the murder of Hawley, as well as the fidelity of the count de Denia's son to Shekel, with whom he was left in pledge for his father's ransom. *Walsingham in Rich.* II. *p.* 216. *Weaver's Funeral Monuments. Sir Robert Cotton's Abridgement, p.* 158.

THAT celebrated poet and philosopher Don Enrique de Villena was his grandson. I have already given a full account of him in another work. See *Letters from an English Traveller in Spain, on the Origin of Poetry in that Kingdom. 8vo.* London, 1781.

DON TELLO DE CASTILLA, brother to Henry, had the lordship of Biscay assigned to him inasmuch as he had married the lady Jane de Lara, heiress of that territory, being daughter of Don John Nunez de Lara and La Cerda, by Maria Diaz de Haro, sixth lord of Biscay. This Don Tello died at Medellin in Estremadura in 1370, without legitimate issue, and not without suspicion of poison. He was interred in the church of

St. Francis in Palencia. The lordſhip of Biſcay devolved to his nephew Don John, afterwards king of Caſtile, and has ever ſince remained in the crown, and belonged to the kings of Caſtile as lords of Biſcay. The lordſhip of Aguilar, with the other eſtates of Don Tello, went to his natural iſſue, from whom many noble families claim their deſcent.

Don Sancho de Castilla, the other brother of Henry, who followed him in all his enterprizes, was by him created count of Alburquerque. He further obtained for him in marriage the Infanta Dona Beatrix, daughter of Peter king of Portugal by Ignez de Caſtro. This match took place at the peace between Spain and Portugal in 1373. The year following Don Sancho was unfortunately murdered in the ſtreets of Burgos, in going out of his houſe to quell a ſcuffle between his domeſtics and thoſe of Don Pedro Gonzales de Mendoza, anceſtor to the duke of Infantado. Don Sancho left an only daughter, heireſs of the county of Alburquerque, and all the great eſtates of her father, on which account ſhe was called "The "rich heireſs of Caſtile." She married her couſin Ferdinand, younger brother to Henry III. king of Caſtile. He became king of Aragon on the demiſe

demiſe without iſſue, of his uncle Martin king of Aragon, and was alſo duke of Penafiel and count of Mayorga.

The county of Alburquerque ſeemed at this period to be the ſport of ſovereigns. It was ſeized by king John II. who gave it to his privado Don Alvaro de Luna, who ſoon after loſt it with his life. In 1464 Henry IV. king of Caſtile erected it into a duchy, in favour of Bertrand de la Cueva; from thence it fell into a French houſe, who continued the name La Cueva.

(Note F, Page 11.)

THAT celebrated Engliſh knight ſir Hugh de Calverley was alſo noticed by Henry after his firſt entrance into Spain, and that he had been crowned at Burgos. He then gave him the lands of Carrion, and made him count thereof; but he loſt them ſoon after at the defeat of Nagera: after which he took the part of King Peter, as the ally of England, and acted under the command of the Prince of Wales. Sir Hugh was the firſt perſon in whoſe favour the county of Carrion had been made

made feudatory and hereditary. Before, it had only been granted for life to the family of Gonzales, who made ſuch a figure in Spain, under the title of the Infantes of Carrion.

WHEN Henry returned from France a ſecond time, he conferred the county of Carrion on his kinſman Don John Sanchez Manuel, ſon of Don Sancho, and grandſon of Don John Manuel, lord of Villena, who had two wives. His firſt was Conſtance, of Aragon, mother to Conſtance, contracted to Alfonſo XI. king of Caſtile, but married to Peter king of Portugal, of whom we have already made mention. See vol. I. page 230. His ſecond wife was Blanche la Cerda, mother to the lady Jane, married to Henry the baſtard, who became king of Caſtile.

(NOTE G, Page 12.)

THE title of duke had been unknown for many ages in Caſtile and Leon; nor is there any mention made of any ſuch in thoſe kingdom in that famous code of laws called *Siete Partidas*, enacted by king Alonſo the Wiſe. In l. 2. tit.

1. of the fecond *Partida*, that King only adds, fpeaking of dukes, that they were invefted by the emperors with confiderable domains called duchies, but fays nothing of Caftile, or there being any fuch in that kingdom; from whence it is implied they were not in ufe; of courfe Henry could not have fallen on a more agreeable project to pleafe the great lords who feconded his efforts to get poffeffion of the crown.

(NOTE H, Page 14.)

AMONG the Caftilians who remained attached to King Peter, the family of Toledo was one of the moft confiderable; though they were ill requited for their loyalty, as appears from his treatment of Gutierre Fernandez de Toledo, commander in chief of his army in Caftile, and his brother Vafco, archbifhop of Toledo, who were fufpected of privately favouring the interefts of Henry.

THE houfe of Toledo deduce their origin from a family of that name, one of the eight chriftian families who preferved their religion in the city of Toledo, when poffeffed by the Moors, and found there

there when the city was taken from the infidels by Alfonso VI. in the eleventh century. — They became favourites under the reign of the Henries, and the princes of that house. John II. in 1439, conferred the town of Alva de Tormes in the kingdom of Leon, with the title of count thereof, on Gutierre Gomez, archbishop of Toledo. He left it by will to his nephew Ferdinand Alvarez de Toledo. who was father of Don Garcias de Toledo, created duke of Alva, in 1469, by Henry IV. king of Castile, who further made him marquis of Coria, and count of Salvatierra. Ever since, they have made a considerable figure in the annals of Spain: one of them has been a knight of the garter. Among others, the severities of the duke of Alva, in Flanders, are universally known. At the beginning of the present century they distinguished themselves by their attachment to the Bourbon family; and contributed in every measure towards their succession to the Spanish dominions, in opposition to the claims of the house of Austria. When the duke of Alva was on his death-bed, and heard of the success of those measures which had been concerted by Cardinal Portocarrero, in opposition to the lord-high-admiral of Castile, and the count de Oropesa, he breathed the following pious ejaculation,

tion, previous to the moment of closing his eyes: "He thanked God that he had seen cardinal Portocarrero go to heaven; the count de Oropesa go to purgatory; and the lord-high-admiral go to the devil." *Alabado sea Dios de que antes de morir tengo el consuelo de ver al Cardinal Portocarrero en la gloria, al Conde de Oropesa en el purgatorio, y al Amirante en el infierno.* "Etat Present de l'Espagne par Veyrac. Amsterdam. 1719."

(Note I, Page 16.)

THE Alcazar, or royal palace in Seville, was originally built by Mahometan princes, after their conquest of Spain. It appears from an Arabic inscription over one of the gates of the palace, that the Nazar, or king of Seville, sent to Toledo about the year 1180 for Jubabi, a capital architect, to serve as a principal director in the construction of this edifice. It afterwards received many embellishments and additions from King Peter, who took great delight in its pleasant situation on the banks of the river Guadalquivir. The great emperor Charles followed his example, and displayed the imperial eagles in the apartments, in testimony of his attachment and affection for this ancient

ancient and venerable building. Naugerius, who was ambaſſador from the republic of Venice to this emperor, though he muſt have ſeen many of the ſumptuous palaces of Italy, ſpeaks of this edifice with greater rapture than it ſeems to deſerve; allowing every merit to its gardens, and bowers of orange and lemon trees, as well as commodious baths, where King Peter ſpent ſo much of his time with the amiable Padilla. The ſaloons are ſpacious, and well-adapted to that ſultry climate, with much gilding and varniſhed tiles, in the Arabeſque manner. When Rodrigo Caro publiſhed his Antiquities of Seville, in 1654, ſpeaking of the hall in this palace, where Peter killed his brother Don Frederic, maſter of the knights of St. James, he adds, that after that tragic event it was called the Hall of the Maſter; and that the ſtains of his blood were then viſible on the pavement. This palace has a particular juriſdiction within itſelf, forming a court at which an alcayde preſides; which is an hereditary office belonging to the dukes of Olivares and St. Lucar, of the illuſtrious houſe of Guzman, who appoint a deputy; who has a vote in the city council, even when the duke is preſent. He has a civil and criminal juriſdiction over thoſe who live within his diſtrict; appoints a treaſurer, ſecretary, head-gardener, and other

other dependents of the palace ; and has a guard of twenty-four halberdiers. An appeal lies from his decrees to the council of war.

Philip V. of Bourbon held his court here after the Succeſſion War which ſecured to him the Spaniſh dominions : and here the treaty of Seville was concluded with Great Britain. His preſent Catholic Majeſty has reſtored this ſtructure to part of its former ſplendor, having aſſigned two ſpacious ſaloons for the aſſemblies of the academy of fine arts lately eſtabliſhed in Seville ; and beſides other elegant ornaments, worthy the magnificence of the donor, the king preſented the academy with many capital pictures of the Spaniſh ſchool, formerly belonging to the jeſuits ; ſuch as thoſe of Ceſpedes, Herrera, Cano, and Valdes. Another apartment is decorated with a collection of plaſter-caſts, from the antique, preſented by the royal academy of San Fernando in Madrid, and various Roman inſcriptions and ſtones relative to the province of Bætica, declaratory of *municipia* not noticed by writers on thoſe ſubjects.

A few years ago, when Cidi Achmet, ambaſſador from the emperor of Morocco, paſſed through palace ;

Seville, he was particularly delighted with this palace; and on perusing the Arabic inscriptions interspersed on the walls, he told Don Francisco Bruna, the deputy alcayde who waited on him, that they contained many points of consequence in the Mahometan religion, and earnestly recommended their preservation.

By a calculation made in the year 1780, the city of Seville, including the suburbs of Triana, contained 11822 houses. Computing five persons to a family, this would only make the population about 59400 souls. When this city was conquered from the Moors by Ferdinand III. after a siege of sixteen months, there went from it, according to the Spanish chronicles, four hundred thousand inhabitants, exclusive of those killed in the siege, and others that remained in the city. Argote de Molina seriously tells us, ancient writers assert, that when the corpse of Ferdinand was interred, angelic voices were heard over his tomb; and that he was reputed a saint, though not canonized, therefore only stiled the holy king Ferdinand, whose holy life is known and revered by numerous miracles. Since that time this king has been canonized by Clement X.

in 1671, who graciously permitted the Spanish nation to celebrate the festival of their new saint.

After having said so much of the alcazar, it must be distinguished from another ancient building near it named the *Alcayceria*, which, in ancient times, served as an exchange, as well as a magazine for depositing of silks and other rich merchandize. The goldsmiths likewise had their shops here; it being a place of safety, walled in, and properly guarded; and had the name of Alcayceria, in allusion to the city of Cesarea in Palestine; with which, and other parts of the East, the city of Seville formerly carried on a considerable trade, when the commerce of the kingdom was chiefly in the hands of the Jews.

(Note H, Page 30.)

THAT "the dead and the absent are bereft "of friends" is a proverb that needs no comment, appears evident; but it is peculiarly applicable to the Castilians, from having been the expression of one of their greatest monarchs, Alfonso the Wise, when he quitted his kingdom, and went to the pope, Nicholas III. to prevail on him to ſupport his election of emperor of Germany, in oppoſition to Richard duke of Cornwall, brother to king Henry III. who had a majority of votes, and was choſen emperor. The king found his endeavours fruitleſs, having moreover put himſelf to great ſtraits by an extraordinary expence: his factious ſubjects took advantage of his abſence to raiſe diſturbances in his kingdom; even his ſon Sancho rebelled againſt him. On which the monarch obſerved, that "the dead "and the abſent never have friends:" *A muertos y a ydos, no ai amigos.*

In the election for the empire, the votes in favour of Alfonſo were thoſe of the archbiſhop of Treves, the duke of Saxony, and the marquis of Brandenburgh, who ſent him ambaſſadors to notify his election, and preſented him with a very curious key of ſingular workmanſhip of different metals, with the arms of the empire and thoſe of Caſtile and Leon engraved thereon, and theſe words: *Dios abrira y el Rei entrara.* "God will "open, and the King will enter." This key is ſtill to be ſeen in the treaſury belonging to the cathedral of Seville.

(NOTE

(Note K, Page 49.)

PHILIP DE CASTRO, a gentleman of Aragon, who followed the fortunes of Henry, ſtood in ſuch high favour, that after the divorce of his ſiſter Jane from Fernando de Caſtro, he gave her in marriage to Philip abovementioned. The conſtant jealouſy which King Peter entertained againſt Henry had been conſiderably increaſed by Fernando de Caſtro's marriage with that lady at Toro, as mentioned in the firſt volume of this work; and the King never reſted till he prevailed on him to divorce her under the pretext of conſanguinity. Henry was ſo watchful of his ſiſter that he traverſed Pedro Carillo, his boſom friend, with a lance, when hunting together; though Carillo had conducted her ſafely to him out of Caſtile, and was ſuppoſed to have been privately married to her.

(Note L, Page 65.)

That the Prince of Wales ſtyled himſelf lord of Biſcay appears from records in the duchy court

 of

of Lancaſter, where it may be found that the Prince, beſide his former titles, likewiſe took upon him thoſe of lord of Biſcay, and of the caſtle of Urdiales; particularly in an inſtrument, bearing date October 8, 1370, 44th Edward III. whereby he grants to his brother John duke of Lancaſter, the caſtle, town and chatellany of *La Roche ſur Yon.* BARNES's *Life of Edward* III.

(NOTE M, Page 71.)

BOCCANEGRA of Genoa had been created high-admiral of Caſtile by king Alfonſo XI. and in 1542 he ſettled the lordſhip of Palma in Andaluſia on his family. Notwithſtanding theſe favours and preference ſhewn him by king Alfonſo, as well as by his ſon King Peter, he joined with Henry againſt him, and ſuffered death in conſequence of his rebellion. His ſon Ambroſe Boccanegra was in favour with Henry after he came to the throne. We find him commanding a Spaniſh fleet, and to have obtained a naval victory over the Engliſh near Rochelle in 1372, when John Haſtings, earl of Pembroke, who was going to ſucceed the duke of Lancaſter in the government of Guyenne, with a ſmall body of forces, was

was taken prisoner with sir Francis Curson, and about sixty English knights. The vessel with the military chest, containing about twenty thousand pounds, was sunk; but the other ships were taken. The English had defended themselves all day with great courage; but the combat being renewed the day following, the Spaniards having forty large carracks well supplied with cannon, which the English wanted, they were obliged to submit to superior force, and the Earl of Pembroke was conducted to Burgos in Castile. According to Smollet, the Spanish fleet was under the direction of one Owen, a Welchman, in the service of France.

(Note N, Page 73.)

THE family of Gusman ordered the ashes of the lady Osorio, and those of Isabella Davalos, to be deposited in a sumptuous marble monument, which was erected in the church of St. Isidore extra Muros, of Seville, the family-vault of the house of Gusman. There may be seen, beautifully sculptured in marble, an elegant figure, representing the lady Osorio, with Isabella Davalos at her feet, covering her with her garments, and performing that pious act in which she sacrificed her life, in token of her unbounded affection and attachment. *Nobleza de Andalusia, par* ARGOTE DE MOLINA. *Sevilla,* 1588.

IN the course of this work, I have already noticed an action of peculiar affection and filial piety, in the case of a son who offered himself, and suffered death at Toledo, to save the life of his aged father. Similar acts of tenderness are not singular in the Spanish nation. As it justly emblazons the generosity of their character, I hope I may be permitted to adduce another instance, though it happened at a later period than the times we are treating of; but whatever serves to exemplify the feelings of the heart in the people I am writing of, may in some degree tend to illustrate their national character.—It is mentioned by Ferdinand del Pulgar, in his Chronicle of the Reign of Ferdinand and Isabel, that on some particular occasion, an officer of the king's army, in order to strike terror into the rebels, had determined to hang six of his prisoners. This engaged a rebel captain named Juan de Berrio, who followed the marquis de Villena, to request he would do the same. The marquis on this ordered his prisoners to draw lots, that six might suffer death. One of those happened to be a gentleman

aged

aged forty-five, who was married, and had ſeveral children. His younger brother, unmarried, was alſo a priſoner, and offered to ſuffer death for his brother, whoſe life was of more conſequence on account of his family. The elder brother ſtrenuouſly refuſed accepting this generous offer, and only requeſted him to remember him to his wife and children. The younger brother ſtill inſiſted on ſuffering; which at laſt was accepted of by the brutal captors, and the younger brother became the victim to his tender regard for his family. The hiſtorian Mariana, while he gives the proper tribute of praiſe to this affectionate brother, and relates the event in a ſimilar manner, has omitted, as well as Pulgar, the name of this enthuſiaſt to fraternal affection: however, by reſearches made in 1555, by order of Philip II. in the town of Villa-nueva, and in the fortreſs of Garcimunoz, where the execution happened, it has been diſcovered that the name of this extraordinary man was John Sainz Telaya; which is proved by original documents relating to the enquiry, depoſited in the royal library of the Eſcurial. *Viage de Eſpana, por* D. ANT. PONZ, *tom.* iii. *Madrid,* 1777.

(Note O, Page 74.)

THE learned and elegant hiſtorian of the emperor Charles V. having made the following obſervation; "I have ſearched in vain among the hiſ-" torians of Caſtile for ſuch information as might " enable me to trace the progreſs of laws and go-" vernment in Caſtle, or to explain the nature of " the conſtitution with the ſame degree of accuracy " wherewith I have deſcribed the political ſtate of " Aragon;" it is with the utmoſt deference that I ſubjoin the following view of the conſtitution of Caſtile; not with a proſpect of offering an exact account of the legiſlation of a kingdom in which the learned writer could not ſee his way ſo clear as he had done in his ſtate of the government of Aragon, but merely as a ſlight ſketch of the juriſprudence of a kingdom, repreſented, by the report of its enemies, to be at that time governed by the mercileſs hand of a tyrant, who knew no other law than his pleaſure, or rule than his wanton paſſion and cruelty.

To attempt a general inveſtigation of the Spaniſh laws, aſcertaining their origin and progreſs, would be an endleſs and Herculean labour. It will

will be ſufficient to mention, that when Spain was ſubject to the Roman emperors, they were either governed by the laws of the *Municipia*, or by the Roman laws, many of which are preſerved to this day. When the Barbarians entered Spain in 420, and divided its provinces among them, they introduced their laws with their dominion. The Goths held them of their king Euric, their firſt legiſlator, who reigned A D. 465; but as the conquering Goths were few in numbers, and the vanquiſhed Spaniards conſiderable, accuſtomed ſo long to the Roman laws, they gave them the liberty of being governed by ſuch laws as they choſe; as appears from Gregory of Tours, *Hiſt. Franc. lib.* 3. *cap.* 13. which privilege remained till the Gothic monarchs, being well eſtabliſhed, gave riſe to the *Fuero Juzgo*, or the Laws of the Judges; being an eminent collection of the laws of the Gothic kings, made by order of king Chindaſvindus, in the firſt year of his reign, A. D. 612. He alſo abrogated the Roman law, and thoſe of any other foreign people. His ſon Receſvindus reviſed them, and added others; to which more were aggregated by his ſucceſſors down to Vitiza; and theſe form that famous code called the FUERO JUZGO.

THE

The *Fuero Juzgo* is the most antient and venerable code of Spanish jurisprudence, and source of legislation; being the first which Spain received from Catholic kings, natives of Spain, and confirmed repeatedly by successive monarchs.

The second origin of Spanish law is the *Fuero Viejo de Castilla*, by command of king Alfonso IX. A. D. 1211, consisting of charters, grants, and customs. It is called *Viejo*, or old, to distinguish it from another code, entitled, *Fuero del Libro de los Concejos de Castilla*, commonly called Fuero Real, ordained by Alfonso the Wise, in 1254.

The third and grand source of jurisprudence, which has been admired by all nations of Europe, is that elaborate system, intitled, *Las Siete Partidas*, which were first drawn up by Ferdinand the Saint, and afterwards perfected by his son, Alfonso the Wise, though they had not the form of law till a long time after, when they were published by king Alfonso XI. in 1347. They were called *Siete Partidas*, in allusion to the seven letters in the name of Alfonso.

OF these two illustrious codes it has been justly observed, that the four books of the FUERO REAL are, as it were, the elements; and the SIETE PARTIDAS, the pandects of Spanish jurisprudence.

THE catholic monarchs Ferdinand and Isabel ordered a new collection of the laws and customs of Castile; which were commented upon by Don Diego Perez in 1556, with the permission and approbation of the great emperor Charles V. his mother Queen Jane being in the city of Toro, March 7, 1505, having also enacted those famous laws which bear the name of that city.

PHILIP II. published a new *Recopilacion* of these laws in Madrid, May 14, 1567; in which it is enacted that all courts should abide by this new code; observing with regard to the *Siete Partidas*, and the *Fuero*, the same regulations as were enforced in the laws of Toro.

PHILIP IV. republished them; including all the new statutes, from 1567 down to 1640. Philip V. of Bourbon did the same, and brought them down to the year 1723; giving this code the title of *Novissima Recopilacion*.

ALL

All the laws contained in these collections which have not been repealed by later ones, are what are sworn to by all judges; and nothing can be alledged in contradiction thereto.

With respect to the civil law, the Goths had a right to annul the Roman law after they extended their dominion in Spain. Chindasvindus did so; which was confirmed by his son, with a heavy fine on those who judged by any other law than the *Fuero Juzgo*. Nor has the civil law been ever since received by any sovereign of Spain. The most we find, is a permission to cite other laws conformable to it; and that in universities it is permitted to be read for greater instruction. The first licence for this purpose is in the *Fuero Real, l.* 5. *tit.* 6. *lib.* 1. The second may be found in the *Ordinanzas Reales* of Alfonso XI. in Alcala, A.D. 1347. and Queen Jane renewed it in the laws of Toro: so that the Roman law has no force, being abrogated by the laws abovementioned. To this we may subjoin the following reflections: The Roman law consists of precepts deduced from the law of nature, the law of nations, and laws purely civil. In those parts which belong to the law of nature and of nations, it ought to be followed; not because it is confirmed by the Roman

law,

law, that has appropriated it to itſelf; but becauſe it is the law of nature and of nations, which is obligatory to mankind, and cannot be annulled by any nation. Touching thoſe regulations which are purely of a civil nature, either they are confirmed by Spaniſh laws, repealed, or paſſed over in ſilence. If they are confirmed, they become law, from the authority of the ſovereign; if they are repealed, they become null, from the nature of the caſe; if paſſed over in ſilence, they are not binding, becauſe the Roman law is in general repealed; and in caſes not mentioned by the law, the ſovereign is the proper legiſlator. By theſe ſtatements we may underſtand the authority of the Roman law in Spain, and in moſt parts of Europe, ſince their repeal; while the greateſt parts of their conſiſtence being founded on the law of nature and of nations, remain neceſſarily inviolable, in the ſame manner as the moſt juſt prohibition of the Koran does not extend to thoſe undeniable principles appertaining to the law of nature comprehended therein.

As for the CANON LAW, the caſe is equally obvious. The pontifical laws either treat of ſpiritual affairs and their dependencies, or of ſuch as are merely temporal. If they relate to ſpirituals

ſpirituals, they are obligatory in Spain, becauſe the general councils, and the ſupreme pontiffs, are acknowledged lawful legiſlators of the poſitive eccleſiaſtical law. If they are merely temporal, they have no force, becauſe the pope is not the ſovereign of Spain, and of courſe not the lawful legiſlator of the Spaniſh monarchy: but it is certain the canon law contains almoſt all the law of nature and of nations; and many of its canons have been transferred to the Spaniſh codes; particularly in the *Siete Partidas,* as king Alfonſo acknowledged. *Part* 1. *tit.* 1. *l.* 6. *Cartas Morales Militares y Civiles recogidas, por* DON GREGORIO MAYANS Y SISCAR. *Madrid,* 1756.

I cloſe theſe remarks with a few obſervations on that great legiſlator Alfonſo X. firnamed the Wiſe, who firſt compoſed that elaborate and immortal work, the *Siete Partidas.* That prince made every effort to improve and govern the kingdom of Caſtile. He employed learned men to draw up the general hiſtory of Spain; and took infinite pains to poliſh the Caſtilian language; for which purpoſe he enacted that all writings and public inſtruments, which heretofore were in Latin, ſhould in future be written in Spaniſh; and for the greater improvement of this plan, he employed

ployed the beſt writers to tranſlate books into that language, in which he laid out above four hundred thouſand ducats. He compoſed thoſe aſtronomical tables which are called Alfonſine in honour of him, and are carefully preſerved in the cathedral of Seville. They were calculated for the meridian of Toledo, as the centre of Spain, and where Alfonſo was born. By theſe the old calendar was regulated, till reformed by Gregory XIII. at the council of Nice. The liberality and generoſity of this great prince is celebrated by hiſtorians. Among other largeſſes he gave one hundred and twenty quintals of ſilver for the ranſom of Baldwin, king of Jeruſalem, taken by the Sultan of Babylon.

Beside the great figure he made in Europe as a legiſlator, he was no leſs active in continuing the wars againſt the Moors, which his father Ferdinand III. had carried on with ſuch ſucceſs. He regained the city of Xerez de la Frontera, in 1264, and peopled it with three hundred *Hidalgos*, whoſe deſcendants flouriſh there to this day. He alſo took the city of Cadiz, and placed three hundred families there; one hundred of *Hidalgos*, which he brought from Old Caſtile, and two hundred of old Chriſtians, who came from the towns of Laredo, Santarder, St. Vincent de la Barqueta, and Caſtro de Urdiales.

RESPECTING the laws of *Behetria*, they have been explained in the firſt part of this work. It remains only to add, that the maſter of St. Bernard, as he was called, who headed that faction, having been taken priſoner by King Peter, at the battle of Nagera, he ordered him to be put to death as a traitor; for which Pope Urban V. excommunicated the King, but ſoon after removed thoſe cenſures. The appellation of maſter of St. Bernard then entirely ceaſed; and thoſe lands, under the ſame name of Behetrias, were annexed to the crown, never to be alienated. They were then new modelled, and had particular privileges annexed to them, and made independent of the inferior tribunals, with an immediate appeal to the King's chancery courts. *Teſoro de la Lengua Caſtillana por Don* SEBASTIAN DE COBARRUVIAS. *Madrid*, 1611.

(NOTE P, Page 75.)

THE Begue de Vilaine, taken priſoner at the battle of Nagera, was another of the baſtard Henry's

Henry's followers, whose services were amply rewarded, having obtained in 1367 a grant of the extensive county of Ribadro, in Galicia. He either sold it again, or, dying without issue, it reverted to the Crown; for it was afterwards disposed of in favour of the constable Ruy Lopez Davalos. This was the last title of count conferred by Henry II.

(NOTE Q, Page 77.)

DE LEYVA returned to Spain with his English wife, and they both ended their days in the province of Rioja in Castile, as appears from the monumental inscriptions over their tomb. They left a son, John Martinez de Leyva, from whom all those of that name were descended; more particularly that celebrated general Don Antonio de Leyva, governor of Milan, and generalissimo in Italy for the emperor Charles V. who in 1530 created him prince of Asculi, marquis of Atela, and count of Monca, with divers other baronies and lordships, which he transmitted to his posterity. *Nobiliario de los Reyes y Titulos de Espana por* ALONSO LOPEZ DE HARO. *Madrid*, 1622.

(Note R, Page 87.)

THE lady Iſabella de la Cerda was the daughter of Don Lewis de la Cerda, by his wife Leonora de Guzman. She was at that time young, and the widow of Don Rodrigo Alvares de Aſturias, by whom ſhe had no children. The baſtard De Bearne was created count of Medina Celi, by Henry, on this marriage; and large eſtates were ſettled on her, on condition of relinquiſhing, for herſelf and her heirs, all pretenſions to the crown of Caſtile, in right of her grandfather Don Alonſo de la Cerda, proclaimed king of Caſtile on the death of his father king Alonſo X. but obliged to yield the ſame to Don Sancho.

Don Lewis de la Cerda, the 5th count of Medina Celi ſprung from the baſtard De Bearne, was created duke of Medina Celi, in 1491, by Ferdinand and Iſabella; and their deſcendants enjoy thoſe honours to this day, with immenſe eſtates.

(Note S, Page 89.)

THAT the Aragonese nation ſhould have produced excellent orators and poets will not appear extraordinary, when we look into their hiſtory, and ſee with what ſedulous attachment they applied themſelves to polite literature, more particularly to poetry; of which many brilliant examples might be adduced about the time we are ſpeaking of: to ſuch a degree, that the hiſtorian Zurita ſays, their talents were ſo far inclined towards theſe purſuits, that the whole kingdom of Aragon, in a manner, became poets; their kings and princes taking the lead, and giving the example. The city of Barcelona was frequently the reſidence of their kings; and the Catalonian language ſo ſoft, that even the Provençal dialect, ſo much admired for its harmony, has been ſuppoſed to proceed from it. It was ſoon after this period, viz. in 1388, that John king of Aragon ſent an embaſſy to Charles VI. requeſting aſſiſtance from the conſiſtory of Toulouſe, to aſſiſt him in founding a ſimilar ſociety in his dominions; which being complied with, and two principal perſons ſent to Barcelona, they formed an eſtabliſhment in that city. Some time paſſed before they were introduced into Caſtile, wherein the marquis of Villena had a conſiderable ſhare, as I have ſtated in another place. *Letters from an Engliſh Traveller in Spain, in* 1778. *London*, 1781.

(Note T, Page 97.)

THIS information relating to the Cortes of Calatonia is derived from the following authority: *Practica Forma y eſtilo de celebrar Cortes en Catalonia. Por* D. Luis de Peguera, *del Conſejo de S. M. Barcelona*, 1632, *4to.* I have not ſeen the original work, but its ſubſtance is inſerted in a learned and curious treatiſe on the antient commerce and marine of Barcelona, entitled, *Memorias hiſtoricas ſobre la marina comercio y artes de la antigua ciudad de Barcelona. Por* Don Antonio de Capmany *y de Montpalceu Individuo de la Real Academia de la Hiſtoria y de los buenas Letras de Sevilla. Madrid*, 1767, 2 vols. *4to.*

The learned author of theſe Memoirs juſt mentioned ſuppoſes that this account of the Cortes of Catalonia had induced Geronimo Blancas, hiſtoriographer of the crown of Aragon, to publiſh his narrative

narrative of the Cortes of that kingdom, entitled, *Modo de proceder en Cortes de Aragon. Zaragoza*, 1641, 4*to*. How far the mode of proceeding of the Cortes of Aragon differs from that of the province of Catalonia I cannot pretend to state with any accuracy, not having seen the book of the historiographer Geronimo Blancas. It is probable the difference is not considerable.

WITH respect to the Cortes of Catalonia, many kings of Aragon held them in person. These assemblies were purely aristocratical till the year 1283, when Peter III. king of Aragon granted a charter to the Commons, with the privilege of sending representatives for the cities and corporations of the province. The emperor Charles V. held the Cortes at Barcelona in 1529. All his successors did the same. The last Cortes were held by Philip V. of Bourbon in 1702.

(NOTE V, Page 104.)

THE town of Madrid made a considerable figure for many ages past in the annals of Castile, though it has not yet been honoured with the title of a city; but it bears the appellation of *Coronada Villa* ever ſince the year 1544; a favour obtained by Don John Hurtado de Mendoza, member for Madrid in the Cortes of Valladolid, who requeſted the emperor Charles, while holding the Cortes, to grant to the place of his nativity, which he had the honour to repreſent, the privilege of bearing a crown over their coat of arms; which the emperor conſenting to, it has been ſtiled "The Crowned Town of Madrid" ever ſince. *Solo Madrid es Corte por* DON ALONSO NUNEZ DE CASTRO, *Croniſta de P. M. Madrid*, 1669.

KING Alonſo VI. finally conquered Madrid from the Moors in the eleventh century. He repaired its edifices, and dedicated the cathedral to the bleſſed Virgin. Since that time Madrid has ever ſignalized itſelf by loyalty and valour, and been frequently the ſeat of the Cortes. Alfonſo XI. father to King Peter, held the Cortes at Madrid in 1327, and always reſided there when he iſſued out ſupplies to the Ricos Hombres and principal commanders of his troops: but that town did not ſeem to pleaſe his ſon King Peter ſo well as his favourite city of Seville; yet the inhabitants, faithful to his dominion, held out the

ſiege

ſiege with great bravery againſt Henry, till the town was betrayed to him by Domingo Munoz, a peaſant, who put him in poſſeſſion of two of the towers; by which means they were obliged to ſurrender to Henry, who held his court there, after he got poſſeſſion of the crown. His ſon king John did the ſame; and what was very remarkable, he ſettled the town and its juriſdiction in fee on Leo king of Armenia, who had come to Madrid, to thank the king for having obtained his liberty of the Sultan of Babylon. The inhabitants were greatly diſguſted at this grant, and during ſix years conſtantly perſiſted in refuſing to accept of Leo as their lord; nor would they acquieſce, till king John ſolemnly promiſed it ſhould revert to the crown after the demiſe of Leo, and never after be alienated. On this they acknowledged king Leo, who confirmed all their privileges, and going to France, died there ſoon after.—Madrid was alſo the firſt to acknowledge the ſovereignty of the emperor Charles, during the life of his mother queen Jane, when there were great diſſentions reſpecting the allowing to Charles the title of king. He repaid their attention with kindneſs, and took great delight in that ſituation, the cool air of which ſeemed congenial to his robuſt and hardy conſtitution. He reſided there, when news was ſent to him that king Francis was taken at the battle of Pavia, who was afterwards brought a priſoner to his court. Philip II. followed the example of the emperor Charles in embelliſhing Madrid, which ſoon became the reſidence of many grandees, and increaſed in its buildings; inſomuch that, in his reign, the number of houſes augmented from two thouſand five hundred to twelve thouſand. Philip III. removed his court to Valladolid in 1601; but many inconveniencies ariſing from this alteration, the court returned again to Madrid in 1605. *Deſcription de la Provincia de Madrid, por D.* THOMAS LOPEZ. *Madrid*, 1763.

NOTWITHSTANDING ſo many great princes have held their court in Madrid, it was only in 1760 that the ſtreets were paved and lighted, with further uſeful improvements, in imitation of other great capitals of Europe; for which they are juſtly indebted to the benevolent reign of his preſent Catholic Majeſty Don Carlos III. With reſpect to the population of this capital, it is far beneath the other great cities of the firſt magnitude in Europe, and little exceeding our populous towns of Mancheſter, Liverpool, and Birmingham.

NOTE

(Note U, Page 115.)

The brave Don Martin Lope de Cordova held out the city of Carmona for ſome time againſt Henry, who laid ſiege to it. At laſt Cordova being in want of proviſions was obliged to ſurrender, on a promiſe of his life given by the king, and confirmed upon oath by Ferdinand, grand maſter of the knights of St. James; but this capitulation was baſely broken by Henry, on ſome frivolous pretence, and Cordova inhumanly put to death in Seville, with as much ſeverity as any of thoſe executions that had happened in the reign of King Peter, of whom Cordova had always been the faithful and loyal ſubject. The maſter of St. James expreſſed great diſguſt at this cruelty, having pledged his honour for the pardon of Cordova, by king Henry's expreſs orders. In this city Peter's two natural children, Don Sancho and Don Diego, were taken priſoners.

(NOTE X, Page 120.)

THE proceedings of the duke of Lancaſter in Spain, relative to his claim on the crown of Caſtile, more properly belong to the reign of Henry II. I ſhall therefore only mention, that he at laſt yielded all further pretenſions to that kingdom, on condition that his daughter Catherine, by Conſtance daughter of King Peter and Maria de Padilla, ſhould eſpouſe the Infante DON HENRY of Caſtile, eldeſt ſon of king John II. by which means the legitimate and illegitimate branches were re-united, and the duke of Lancaſter's grandſon HENRY III. ſucceeded to the throne of Caſtile.

IT was further agreed on at this match, that the Infante Don Henry and the ſucceſſive eldeſt Infantes, heirs apparent to the crown, ſhould be ſtiled PRINCES OF ASTURIAS, in imitation of the Engliſh faſhion with reſpect to the Prince of Wales.

THE province of Aſturias had the preference on this occaſion to other more conſiderable domains, in conſideration of its being the firſt that

had

had a Christian king after the invasion of the Saracens, and whose inhabitants so valiantly defended themselves against them. It is further remarkable, that as the title of Prince of Wales first took place on the marriage of Edward, eldest son of Henry III. king of England, with Eleanor of Castile, daughter of Ferdinand III. that of Prince of Asturias had its rise on the nuptials of Henry of Castile, afterwards king Henry III. with Catherine of Lancaster.

When the duke of Lancaster went to Portugal, during his strife in support of his Spanish claim, he took with him his daughter Philippa, by his former wife the lady Blanche, daughter of Thomas duke of Lancaster, and sister to Henry IV. king of England. This lady he disposed of in marriage to the Bastard of Portugal, king John I. who was made a knight of the garter on the occasion, and ever after used for his crest and supporters the winged dragon, with the invocation to St. George, whose figure on horseback is carried about in processions in Lisbon, as a tutelar saint of the kingdom of Portugal. The king of Aragon likewise claims the protection of our good St. George, whose cross and banner was borne by Raymond count of Barcelona

celona in the tenth century, in teſtimony of the tutelar aſſiſtance of this magnanimous ſaint againſt the infidels. The republic of Genoa value themſelves on the ſame interceſſion and patronage.

By the alliances above-mentioned, the duke of Lancaſter having diſpoſed of his daughters, and made them both queens, relinquiſhed all further thoughts of the realm of Caſtile. The illuſtrious blood of LANCASTER, in a courſe of ages, diffuſed itſelf univerſally through the nobility of Spain and Portugal; in both which kingdoms they continue to bear the name of Lancaſter, and evince that noble deſcent with a diſtinguiſhed and peculiar predilection.

(NOTE Y, Page 120.)

THE pleaſure of the chace was a paſſion in which Peter followed the ſteps of his father king Alfonſo XI. whoſe affection for hunting was ſo great, that he could not even refrain from it at the ſiege of Algeziras; and would ſteal moments to quit his camp, purſuing this diverſion with ſuch imprudence, that he once narrowly eſcaped

being

being taken by a ſtraggling party of Moors. The Carthuſian convent of *Las Cuevas*, in the ſuburbs of Seville, poſſeſſes an elegant and valuable manuſcript of king Alfonſo, on the art of hunting, embelliſhed with a great variety of portraits of the principal perſonages of the court, in the dreſſes of the times, with repreſentations of the implements uſed in hunting the beaſts of the foreſt. It contains one hundred and eighty-five leaves; and on the firſt is written, *Eſte libro mandamos facer nos el noble Rey Don Alonſo que fabla en todo loque pertenece a la Manera de la Monteria.*

Among the different modes of the chace, that of falconry has ever been prevalent, and held in the higheſt eſteem by the kings of Caſtile and of Portugal. Diego Fernandez de Ferreira, in his treatiſe on that ſport, ſays, that Ferdinand king of Portugal uſed always to keep three hundred falcons of different ſorts; but that it dwindled greatly after the death of king Sebaſtian. According to Guicciardini, it was brought firſt into Italy from the northern nations by the emperor Frederic Barbaroſſa; however, as it has always been in eſteem among the Arabs and Perſians, it may be preſumed to be of a higher antiquity. Diego Ferreira further adds, that the wild Arabs

of

of Africa were remarkably fond of that diverſion, and always went armed with a lance and ſhield, carrying a falcon on their ſhoulders as an emblem of gentility. Modern nations have continued the ſame idea. The king's falconer is generally a principal officer of the court, and the repreſentations of them in armorial bearings followed the introduction of heraldry, and were conſidered as honourable badges, intended to denote an ancient and noble origin, and granted in conſequence to ſeveral conſpicuous families. Among the reſt the noble family of Dillon Earl of Roſcommon, in the kingdom of Ireland, have for ſeveral ages paſt bore for a creſt to their arms, a falcon riſing, *pearl* beaked legged, and belled *topaz*, on a chapeau *ruby*.

As the names of theſe falcons frequently occur in peruſing the antient chronicles, and afford a variety of metaphorical alluſions, I beg leave to ſubjoin a deſcription of their different ſorts, in further illuſtration of the cuſtoms of thoſe times. The Spaniſh falconers reckoned eight ſorts of falcons, viz. the SACRE, GIRIFALTE, NIEBLE, BAHARI, ALFANIQUE, TAGAROTE, AZOR, and BORNI.

SACRE,

SACRE.

THE moſt valuable ſpecies of falcons are called by this name not only by the Spaniards, but alſo by the French and Engliſh, as well as in Latin, and are thought to have derived that name from being termed by Virgil *ſacer ales*. Æn. lib. II. v. 127.

> Quem facile accipiter ſaxo ſacer alis ab alto,
> Conſequitur pennis ſublimem in nube columbam.

The Romans probably derived the appellation from the Greeks, who called it ιεραξ, *ſacer avis*. Furretiere calls it Britannicus.

GIRIFALTE.

THE ger falcon, ſo called by Juan Lopez Velaſco, *ſeu gerens falcem*, from the ſhape and government of his pounces; or *girifalcone* by the Italians, from the verb *giro*; alluding to his planeing the air, and the circles he performs, before he darts on his prey. There is little difference between the *ſacre* and the *girifalte*.

NIEBLI,

NIEBLE,

So called *quasi nebulæ*, from their high flight as it were among the clouds. They are likewise said to be so called, from their having been first discovered near the town of Niebla, in the days of king Bamba, the father of fable, like our good king Arthur. They generally let the *nieble* fly at herons. The beautiful Inez de Castro, mentioned in this work, was called *cuello de garza*, or heron-neck, on account of her taper and elegant form.

BAHARI.

THIS appellation is understood to have an Arabic original, and to answer the word *ultra-marine*; the first having been brought from very remote parts beyond seas.

ALFANIQUE,

So called from a Hebrew word of a similar sound, implying *docile* and *gentle*, to denote their great facility in being taught and instructed for the sport. They come from the kingdom of

Tremecen

Tremecen in Africa, and are generally let fly at hares and partridges.

TAGAROTE.

These are brought from the mountains that lay near the river Tagaros in Africa, and are found in great numbers. They are remarkable for fiercenefs, and faftening on their prey. It is alfo a nick-name for thofe poor gentlemen who become fpungers, and fix themfelves wherever they can find a maintenance.

AZOR.

I am unacquainted with the origin of this name; but as many of thefe birds were found in the Weftern Iflands by the Portugueze, when they firft difcovered them, in the reign of Alfonfo V. they called the iflands by the name of *Azores*, from the hawks which they found there.

BORNI.

THESE are ſo called on account of their coming from a diſtrict of that name on the coaſt of Guinea in Africa.

To deſcribe the different qualities of theſe birds the Spaniſh falconers ſay:

Alas de Niebli;
Corazon de Bahari;
Cuerpo y cola de Girifalti;
Ojo y viſta de Borni;
Preſſa y garra de Sacre;
Seguridad de Alfanique;
Y riſa de Tagarote.

ANOTHER writer ſays:

Alas de Niebli;
Corazon de Bahari;
Cabeza de Borni;
Manos de Sacre;
Cuerpo de Girifalte;
Ojos de Alfanique;
Pico de Tagarote.

That is, "The flight of the Niebli; the courage of the Bahari; the head of the Borni; the "pounce

"pounce of the Sacre; the body of the Giri-"falte; the eye of the Alfanique; the bill of "the Tagarote."

See the following curious books—

Arte de Caza de Alteneria, por FERNANDEZ FERREIRA. *Lisboa*, 1616. 4*to.*

Origen de la Caza, por JUAN MATHEOS. *Madrid*, 1634. 4*to.*

Arte de Ballisteria y Monteria, por ALONSO MARTINEZ DE ESPINAR. *Madrid, en la emprenta Real*, 1644. 4*to.*

THIS curious book, which is dedicated to the Infante Don Carlos, whose portrait is affixed to it, has likewise many other plates, and is in the king of France's library.

(NOTE Z, Page 121.)

THE singular asperity of expression of the historian Matheo Villani induces me to annex the original text, wherein he calls Peter, "crudelissimo e bestiale Re—che tutto l'animo

"Reale cambio in crudele tirannia---forſenato Re "---perverſo tirano di Spagna, non degno d'eſſere "nomato Re."

Smollet calls Peter "a brutal monſter, who "ought to have been hunted down as the foe of "the human kind."

And Roderic Sanchez, biſhop of Palencia, with equal ſeverity, has alſo ſaid, "Clamabat ad ſupe-"ros tanta hominis ſævitia adeo ut ſicut ſcriptura "commemorat, ad cœlos pertingeret tanta cru-"delitas, et quia ſcriptum eſt, crudelis propin-"quos abjicit, ſuſcitavit Deus contra eum pro-"pinquos ipſos." Part iv. cap. 17.

SUPPLEMENT:

CONTAINING OBSERVATIONS ON THE MARITIME COMMERCE OF CASTILE AND ARAGON.

COMPARED WITH THAT OF ENGLAND, AT THE PERIOD OF THIS HISTORY.

CONSIDERING the preceding work as not merely confined to trace the cataſtrophe of the unfortunate Peter, King of Caſtle and Leon; but moreover intended to exemplify the manners of the age; I have already, as a further illuſtration of the times, annexed a tranſient view of the arts and manufactures, as well as the ſtate of commerce in the Mediterranean, with reſpect to the two rival powers of Caſtile and Aragon. To this ſtatement it ſeems a natural progreſſion to offer a few words concerning the ſettlement and mercantile tranſactions of the Spaniards in England, with which I ſhall cloſe my obſervations on that period of hiſtory. I am indebted for theſe details to that enlightened Academician Don Antonio de Campmani, whoſe Memoirs on the Commerce of Barcelona I have already had occaſion to mention with great ſatisfaction. Without following literally what he has ſaid on this head, the reader will conſider the ſubject - matter of this information as ariſing from that learned and well-informed writer, whom I have not followed literally, nor merely as a tranſlator; while I readily acknowledge the extent of the obligation, of which I claim no other merit than transferring its ſubſtance into our language.

THE mercantile ſpirit, he aſſerts, which animated the different ſtates of the Mediterranean to make long voyages, and frequent the ports of England and Flanders, was conſpicuous

ſpicuous in the 15th century, and no where with more activity than among the Spaniards. With reſpect to England, moſt of the trade was carried on there by foreigners; ſuch as the Lombards, the Hans Towns, and the Catalonians, who enriched themſelves by the activity of their commerce, being the carriers of their products and ſuperfluities, and taking home returns in their own veſſels.

THE firſt treaty of commerce of the Engliſh, according to their own hiſtorians, was about the year 1217, with Haquin king of Norway; but the Engliſh did not venture to trade there with their own ſhips till the beginning of the fourteenth century. Nor was their flag known in the Mediterranean till the end of the enſuing century; though according to Anderſon, in his Hiſtory of Commerce, they had lately become acquainted, and were admitted into the ports of Caſtile and Portugal. However it is evident, that the firſt ſettled trade of England in the Levant is not of a higher date than the beginning of the ſixteenth century.—In the year 1511, and the following, and in 1534, a fleet of merchant-ſhips from London, Southampton, and Briſtol, failed for Sicily, Candia, Cyprus, Scio, Tripoli, and Baruth, and opened a trade for their cloth, cotton ftuffs, and other wares, bringing back in return Greek wines, camblets, filks, oil, cotton, and carpets. But the direct trade to Conftantinople, and other ports of Turkey, was not known to them before the year 1599, nor to the Dutch till 1612, at which period the States-General of the United Provinces made their firft treaty of commerce with the Grand Signior.

How different is the prefent fituation of England! Prior to the reign of Edward III. all their raw wool (fuch fmall quantities excepted as were worked up for abfolute ufe at home) was fold to the Flemings and Lombards, who were the carriers, and difperfed it over Europe. Notwithftanding the pains taken by Edward III. to increafe his manufactures at home, by inviting weavers from Flanders to fettle in his dominions, ftill a long time paffed before the Englifh fent their own manufactures to foreign markets; fo that the exportation of wool remained a confiderable branch of their commerce; and according to the reprefentations of Hume, the manufactures of England in 1327 were in a very backward and unimproved ftate, and in no degree comparable with the ingenuity and induſtry of the Flemings.

THE bad policy of England at that time will evince the ſlow progreſs of their manufactures. During the whole courſe of the fourteenth century, they had no other exports than raw wool, leather, butter, tin, and lead, and a few other raw materials; wool being the chief export, of which, one year with another, there were ſent abroad about thirty thouſand ſacks, which, at five pounds ſterling each, amounted to one hundred and fifty thouſand of that currency; which would be, according to the preſent value of money, four hundred and fifty thouſand pounds. Beſide theſe conſiderations, many others militated againſt the increaſe of their commerce. Edward, it is true, had encouraged foreign workmen, and prohibited the wear of other articles but ſuch as were made in his dominions; yet the parliament prohibited the exportation of their own manufactures; which, beſide being a check upon their foreign trade, implied a groſs contradiction, ſince they ſtill permitted the exportation of wool. Another act was made in 1377, equally repugnant to national induſtry; that

that was, the prohibiting the exportation of iron.

TILL that time their measures seemed fatal to commerce, and inauspicious to every branch of its progress. In 1264, Henry, eldest son of the earl of Leicester, who had usurped the crown, made a monopoly of all the wools of England, the only valuable article that supported any trade against their rivals. On the other hand, the inhabitants of the Cinque Ports abandoned themselves during those troubles to the most flagrant acts of piracy: they plundered and burnt the ships of all nations that came within their reach, and murdered their crews; so that their coasts were deserted, and no traders would venture to enter their ports. This made the price of foreign articles rise to an immoderate height; and the English being ignorant of the art of dyeing, were obliged to wear their cloth in its first rude state, at so low a pitch was industry and ingenuity at that time amongst them.

To these impediments may be added the tyranny of the feudal laws, the intestine divisions in the kingdom, the irruption of the Danes, and other northern pirates; all which tended to co-

ver

ver the iſland with the veil of barbariſm and ignorance. The continuation of their broils after the Norman Conqueſt, their wars in France in ſupport of their poſſeſſions, and claims on the remainder, were invincible obſtacles to a regular ſyſtem of commerce, no leſs than the diviſions of the houſes of York and Lancaſter, which deluged the kingdom in blood till the end of the fifteenth century; ſo that the Engliſh nation were the laſt to acquire a proper ſyſtem of national commerce, and avail themſelves of the advantages ariſing from induſtry and their inſular ſituation.

The navigation from the Mediterranean to England, which firſt began about the end of the thirteenth century, muſt have been extremely hazardous, as well from the length of the voyage, as from the entrance of the Channel at a time when navigation was ſo imperfect; excluſive of the depravity of the Engliſh, who wanted to trade to foreign ports, but would not ſuffer foreigners to come peaceably to theirs. The annals of the fourteenth century abound with records and letters of the kings of England to the ſovereigns of Caſtile, France, Portugal, Aragon, and Majorca, and to the republics of Venice and Genoa, giving ſatisfactory anſwers to the complaints of of thoſe powers, for the repeated inſults offered by Engliſh ſhips to the veſſels of thoſe ſtates that frequented their ports, or went to thoſe of Flanders. Amongſt many others which we ould offer, we ſhall only produce the following.

In 1333 Edward III. wrote to Alonſo IV. king of Aragon, who had given letters of repriſals to his ſubjects, to indemnify them for the damages they had ſuffered in the Channel by Engliſh veſſels, which had plundered them of their effects, that he could not be anſwerable for the unwarrantable acts of independent pirates.

In 1336 the Genoeſe petitioned for the reſtitution of a valuable cogg, loaded with rich merchandize from the Eaſt, of the value of fourteen thouſand four hundred marks ſterling, which had been plundered in the Channel by the commander of an Engliſh ſquadron, contrary to the ſafe-conduct granted to the republic.

As a further proof of the conſequence of the trade carried on by the Catalonians in the Mediterranean, their records prove that, even in 1331, the

the port of Barcelona could fit out veſſels of three decks, with five hundred men on board, and various caſtles on their decks. The original contract for ſuch a veſſel is ſtill extant in their archives, in which the articles of agreement are ſtated between the magiſtrates of Barcelona on the one part, and three merchants on the other; in which the latter let out to hire a large cogg, fitted out as a privateer, to cruize againſt the Genoeſe, and to carry five hundred men. Among other ſtores ſhe had three thouſand one hundred and ſixty-ſix new arrows, forty large ſpears, three hundred and fifty-ſeven middle-ſized ſpears, ſixteen pikes for boarding the enemy, three hundred croſs-bows, ſixty-eight paveys, forty-nine new helmets and fifty-ſeven old ones, forty-two cuiraſſes, forty-three gorgets, ſeventeen cheſts of bows and arrows, fourteen anchors, ſix pair of colours, fifty-three oars, with an infinite number of warlike ſtores, to the amount of ſeven thouſand five hundred and twenty articles.

In 1352 the ſame king Edward was obliged to give ſatisfaction to the ſenate of Piſa, for one of their ſhips taken by a pirate on the coaſt of Sandwich. Rymer furniſhes in every page a variety of inſtances of ſimilar conduct on the part of a nation,

nation, which, though at that time ferocious and inhoſpitable, has ſince, not only humanized itſelf in a ſuperior degree, but given laws to the arts and to political refinement, as well as to patriotiſm, and introduced wiſdom and philoſophy into their ſenate.

The Spaniards were not behind-hand in availing themſelves of the ignorance and rudeneſs of the Engliſh. They had even formed eſtabliſhments in England ſo early as the cloſe of the thirteenth century; for when the famous Aſſembly of Arbitrators was convened in London in 1303, as mentioned in Coke's Inſtitutes, (Inſtitute IV. page 142.) to decide on the differences between king Edward and Philip the Fair of France, reſpecting the dominion of the channel, we find, among the different arbitrators then ſettled in England, who were added to the biſhops, lords, and others appointed for the purpoſe, the Spaniſh merchants were equally nominated. Before this period we find, under Edward II. that the Spaniards are particularly taken notice of in the charter granted by that prince, mentioned by Rymer, tom. II. part iii. p. 15. for foreigners of different nations to trade in his dominions; though this licence was only allowed

allowed to them as wholesale traders, and not to open shops, spices and grocery excepted, which they might deal in by retail. It does not appear that the Spaniards thus settled in England had Consuls for the protection of their trade, but that all differences arising in the fairs and markets were settled by a jury composed of a certain number of foreigners and natives, who judged of the same according to the laws and customs of the land,----the particular documents of which are specified in the Fœdera.

From hence we may draw a fair conclusion of the share of the spice trade, which the Spaniards carried on in England at that time in competition with the Venetians and Genoese, which will shew the activity of their merchants, and how well adapted the mercantile spirit was to their character, industrious habits, and pursuits.

It is allowed that the Florentines were the first bankers and negotiators who got possession of all money transactions; but returns in those days were generally made by barter, and foreigners carried off the raw materials of the country, which the inexperience of the English pre-

vented

vented them from working up into manufactures in their own country.

Wool being the principal ſtaple of the kingdom from the thirteenth century, the Engliſh were ſo little verſed in the principles of commerce, that the fairs for the ſale of this article were held out of their own country, and kept in the city of Antwerp in Brabant, which was the general warehouſe and depoſit where the Engliſh factors tranſacted their buſineſs. It was afterwards removed to St. Omer's, from whence they uſed to reſort to the famous fairs of Liſle in Flanders; and finally, in 1348, under Edward III. who was not much wiſer than his predeceſſor, the general ſtaple was removed to Calais, where the Engliſh diſpoſed of their wool, hides, tin, leather, and ſuch few manufactured goods as they were able to execute; the makers not even underſtanding the policy of fixing the ſtaple at home, and drawing every advantage from the influx of foreigners, and competition among themſelves, to the general advantage and benefit of the kingdom.

In the fifteenth century the merchants of Aragon purſued their trade with England with no leſs vigour

vigour than heretofore. In the firſt place, Henry V. ordered letters patent to be made out, in 1418, in favour of the ſubjects of the crown of Aragon who ſhould come into his ports with their veſſels and merchandize, allowing them ſafe-conduct, and every kind of protection and comfort. Their commerce with England muſt have been conſiderable, and their purchaſes of wool very great, as they were at that time experienced manufacturers, and dexterous in making ſuperfine cloth; more particularly the citizens of Barcelona; of whom a record is ſtill extant of 1446, wherein the magiſtrates of that city ſent inſtructions to their agent in London to purchaſe four hundred quintals of the fineſt wool, in which the prices and qualities are particularly adverted to, with directions to buy the ſame ten per cent. cheaper than the former year; and that, to prevent deception, the wool was to remain on account of the ſeller, from the time of ſhipping till it was unloaded in Barcelona.

In confirmation of the above fact, the municipal archives of Barcelona are poſſeſſed of a record, relating to the return of a galleaſs from London to Barcelona, laden with two hundred and fifty ſacks of wool, which were diſtributed to different manufacturers, to be made up into cloth, and ſent back to England for ſale.

Among the ſubſidies granted by parliament to Henry VI. in 1453, there was a tax of ſixteen ſhillings on every foreigner ſettled in England, and ſix ſhillings upon travellers, who went into different parts of the country. The Catalonians ſtill purſued their mercantile ſyſtem there; but they probably dwindled towards the cloſe of that century, when the Engliſh began to attempt a navigation in the Mediterranean with their own veſſels. By a treaty agreed on between Henry VII. and the Republic of Florence in 1490, it was ſtipulated, that none but Engliſh ſubjects ſhould henceforward import wools in their own bottoms into the territories of the republic; and that the ſtaple ſhould be held in the port of Piſa; in conſequence of which, it was ſettled that no foreigner ſhould export wool from England, except the Venetians; to whom this favour waa granted, as may be ſeen in Rymer, to ſerve them in part return of their annual fleets; and therefore they were allowed to carry away ſix hundred ſacks only as a ſupply for their own manufactures.

From

From that period the English ſhipping began to extend itſelf, and their merchants explored ſeas and harbours where hitherto their flag had not been known; yet in Henry VIII.'s time their direct commerce northward did not extend itſelf further than the coaſts of Flanders and its appurtenances. The merchants of thoſe States bought the goods of the Engliſh, and diſperſed them over Germany, which held the Flemings in a kind of dependency on the Engliſh. When it happened to be broken in 1520, the Flemings were forbidden from purchaſing the manufactures of England. The conſequence was fatal to England: Manufactures declined; indigence and mutiny followed in different parts of the kingdom; the foreign workmen were more expert than the Engliſh: animoſities aroſe to a ſtill higher pitch againſt all ſtrangers who had obtained a ſettlement amongſt them. Their numbers were ſo great, according to Hume, that when Henry VIII. ordered them to quit the kingdom, fearful of their attachment to queen Catherine, they conſiſted of fifteen thouſand people.

In proof of the backwardneſs of the Engliſh trade, compared with that of the Spaniards at the period now under conſideration, it is apparent from records, that, while the Castilians and Aragonese had various treaties of commerce with foreign potentates, the English had no treaty for that purpose with any European power or state, prior to the first mentioned under queen Mary with the Czar of Muscovy, to open a communication with Archangel. In Elizabeth's days, manufactures were in general of such inferior taste and workmanship, that foreign goods were in a manner constantly preferred. In 1567, the same historian (Hume) informs us, that, in London alone, the number of foreign workmen amounted to four thousand eight hundred and fifty people, of different nations, of which three thousand eight hundred and thirty-eight were Flemings, and only fifty-eight Scotchmen. The religious persecutions, which followed soon after in France and Flanders, drove numberless artists into England, which furnished them an asylum; the arts began to flourish, manufactures were established, and increased to an amazing degree.

Such was the state of commerce in England, apparently inferior in policy and extent, for a century previous and successive to that of Castile and Aragon, at the period of Peter the Cruel.

The

The discovery of America changed the face of affairs. The enterprising genius of Cromwell gave further animation to the British flag; the Act of Navigation covered the seas with her shipping, and in half a century she performed wonders. The spirit of liberty and commerce established at the Revolution, raised the British empire to a state of glory unparalleled in history; her senators were admired for their dignity, moderation, and wisdom; her fountains of justice were celebrated for their purity; and her affluent citizens in a manner engrossed the trade of the world.

LIST

OF

SPANISH BOOKS

CONSULTED IN THE COURSE OF THIS WORK.

CRONICA del Rey Don Pedro, Rey de Castilla y de Leon, por Don Pedro Lopez de Ayala, Chanciller Mayor de Castilla. Con las enmiendas del Secretario Geronimo Zurita; y las correctiones y notas anadidas, por Don Eugenio de Llaguno Amirola, Caballero de la orden de Santiago, de la Real Academia de la Historia. *Madrid*, 1779. 4to.

Cronica de Don Pedro Nino Conde de Buelna, por Gutierre Diez de Games, su Alferez—La publica Don Eugenio de Llaguno Amirola, Caballero de la orden de Santiago, de la Real Academia de la Historia. *Madrid*, 1782. 4to.

Nobiliario

Nobiliario Genealogico de los Reyes y Titulos de Eſpana dirigido a la mageſtad del Rey Don Philipe IV. compueſto por Alonzo Lopez de Haro, criado de ſu Mageſtad y miniſtro en ſu Real Conſejo de las ordenes. Con privelegio en Madrid, por Luis Sanchez, Impreſſor Real. 1ma y 2da parte. *Madrid*, 1622. Folio.

*** Of this work Langlet de Freſnoy, in his Catalogue of Hiſtorians, makes the following obſervation: "Quoique par un decret du "Conſeil Royal de Caſtile, on a voulu porter attente au credit de ce livre, il s'eſt ſoutenue malgre cela contre toute oppoſition, "et eſt fort eſtime des ſavants."

Nobleza de Andaluſia al Catholico Rey Don Philipe N. S. Rey de las Eſpanas, &c. por Gonçalo Argote de Molina. *Sevilla*, 1588. Folio.

Deſcripcion de la Provincia de Madrid, por Don Thomas Lopez, Penſioniſta de S. M. y de la Real Academia de San Fernando. *Madrid*, 1769. 12mo.

Cartas Morales, Militares, Civiles, et Literarias, de varios Autores Españoles, recogidas y publicadas por Don Gregorio Mayans y Siſcar. 2 tomos. *Madrid*, 1756.

Memorias Hiſtoricas ſobre la marina comercio y artes de la antigua ciudad de Barcelona publicadas por diſpoſicion y a expenſas de la real junta y conſulado de comercio de la miſma ciudad, y diſpueſtas por Don Antonio de Campmany y de Montpalau, individuo de la Real Academia de la Hiſtoria y de la de Buenas Letras de Sevilla. *Madrid*, 1779. 2 tomos en 4to.

Origen de las Dignidades Seglares de Caſtilla y Leon, con Relacion Sumaria de los Reyes de eſtos Reynos, de ſus Acciones, Caſamientos, Hijos, Muertes, Sepulturas. Por el Doctor Salazar de Mendoza. Con Licencia en la imprenta Real. *Madrid*, 1657, Folio.

Memorias para la Hiſtoria de la Poeſia y Poetas Eſpanoles dadas a luz por el Monaſterio de S. Martin, de Madrid. Obra Poſthuma del Rmo. P. M. Fr. Martin Sarmiento, Benedictino,

dedicada

dedicada al Exmo. Sr. Duque de Medina Sidonia. *Madrid*, 1775. 8vo.

Advertencias a la Hiſtoria del Padre Juan de Mariana, de la Compania de Jeſus, impreſa en Toledo, en Latin, ano de 1592, y en Romance el de 1601, en que ſe enmienda gran Parte de la Hiſtoria de Eſpana. A Don Bernardino Fernandez de Velaſco, Condeſtable de Caſtilla y Leon, por Pedro Mantuano, ſu Secretario. En *Madrid*, en la imprenta Real. 1613.

Reſtablecimento de las Fabricas y Comercio Eſpanol, ſu autor Don Bernardo de Ulloa, Gentilhombre de Boca de S. M. Alcayde Mayor del Cabildo de la Ciudad de Sevilla, y al preſente ſu Procurador Mayor in eſta Corte, dedicado al Rey nueſtro Senor. *Madrid*, 1740. 12mo.

Coleccion de Poeſias Caſtillanas Anteriores al Siglo XV. &c. Illuſtrada con Notas por D. Thomas Antonio Sanchez, Bibliothecario de S. M. *Madrid*, 1779, 8vo.

Origines de la Lengua Eſpanola, compueſta por varios Autores; recogidas por Don Gregorio Mayans,

Mayans y Siſcar, Bibliothecario del Rey nueſtro Senor. 2 tomos, en *Madrid*, 8vo. 1737.

Dialogos de las Armas y Linages de la Nobleza de Eſpana. Por Don Antonio Aguſtin Arzobiſpo de Tarragona, obra poſthuma, cotejado con varios Libros aſſi Manuſcritos como Impreſſos, por Don Gregorio Mayans y Siſcar, Bibliothecario del Rey nueſtro Senor. *Madrid*, 1734.

Ilici, hoi la Villa de Elche. Illuſtrada con varios Diſcurſos; ſu Autor Don Juan Antonio Mayans y Siſcar, Preſbitero. *Valencia*, 1771.

*** *I am indebted to my worthy friend Don* Juan Antonio Mayans, *canon of the cathedral of Valencia, author of the above treatiſe, for the information therein contained reſpecting the kingdom of Valencia; which very ingenious treatiſe he did me the favour to preſent me in* 1777, *when I had the pleaſure to ſee him in the City of Valencia, at the houſe of his brother Don* Gregorio Mayans, *for whoſe politeneſs and civility I have already expreſſed, and am happy to renew, my ſinckreſt acknowledgments.*

Viage

Viage de Eſpana, en que ſe da noticia de las coſas mas apreciables y dignas de ſaberſe que hay en ella. Por Don Antonio Ponz, Secretario de la Real Academia de San Fernando, dedicado al Principe nueſtro Senor. *Madrid*, 1776.

Cronica de Don Alonſo el onceno de eſte nombre de los Reyes que reynaron en Caſtilla y Leon, conſorme a un antiguo MS. de la Real Biblioteca del Eſcurial y otro de la Mayanſiana. Iluſtrada con apendices y varios documentos. Por Don Franciſco Cerda y Rico, Oficial de la Secretario de Eſtado y del Deſpacho Univerſal de Indias, Academico del numero de la Real Academia de la Hiſtoria. *Madrid*, 1787, 4to.

Diſcurſos de la Nobleza de Eſpana al Rey Don Philipe IV. Por Bernabe Moreno de Vargas, Regidor perpetuo de la Ciudad de Merida. *Madrid*, 1622.

Tratado de la Nobleza, Titulos y Ditados de Eſpana. Por Juan Benito Guardiola. *Madrid*, 1591, 4to.

Teſoro de la Lengua Caſtillana o Eſpanola, compueſta por el Licenciado Don Sebaſtian de Cobarruvias Oroſco, Capellan de ſu Mageſtad, dirigido a la Mageſtad Catolica del Rey Don Felipe III. nueſtro Senor. *Madrid*, 1611, Folio.

Hiſtoria del Reino de Portugal, por Manuel de Faria y Souſa, Caballero del Habito de Chriſto. *Amberes*, 1730, Folio.

Nobiliarcha Portugueza, Tratado da Nobreza hereditaria y politica, eſcrita por Antonio de Villaſboas y Sampayo. *Liſboa*, 1676.

Los Quarenta Libros de la Cronicas de todos los Reynos de Eſpana. Por Eſtevan de Garibay. *Barcelona*, 1628, Folio.

Hiſtoria General de Eſpana. Por el Padre Juan de Mariana, de la Compania de Jeſus. *Madrid*, 1780.

Antiguidades y Principado de la Iluſtriſſima Ciudad de Sevilla, dirigida al Excelentiſſimo

Senor

Senor Don Gaſpar de Guzman, Conde Duque de San Lucar la Mayor, por el Dr. Don Rodrigo Caro. *Sevilla*, 1634, Folio.

Refianes o Proverbios que coligio y gloſſo el Comendador Hernan Nunez, Profeſſor de Retorica y Griego en la Univerſidad de Salamanca. *Lerida*, 1621, 4to.

La Filoſofia vulgar de Juan de Mallara, vezino de Sevilla, a la C. R. M. del Rey Don Filipe, que contiene mil refranes gloſſadas. —— Van juntamente las quatro cartas de Blaſco de Garay, hechas en refranes para enſenar el uſo dellos. *Lerida*, 1621.

Anales de la Corona de Aragon. Por Geronimo Zurita. *Sarragoſſa*, 1618.

Las Siete Partidas del Rey Don Alfonſo el Sabio Gloſſadas, por el Sr. Don Gregorio Lopez, del Conſejo Real de las Indias. *Por el Dr. Don Joſeph Berni y Catala*, Abogado de los Reales Conſejos. Con Real Privilegio. VALENCIA, 1767, Folio.

Sumario

Sumario de los Reyes de Efpana. Por el Defpenfero Mayor de la Reyna D. Leonor Muger del Rey Don Juan I. de Caftilla, con las alteraciones y adiciones que pofteriormente le hizo un anonymo. Publicado por D. Eugenio de Llaguno Amirola, Caballero de la orden de Santiago, &c. *Madrid*, 1781.

INDEX

TO THE

SECOND VOLUME.

Where *n* occurs before the paginal reference in a parenthesis, thus (*n*), the reader is requested to turn to the Notes and Illustrations. Where an asterisk is prefixed, reference must be had to the passages so marked.

A.

Alfonso

I N D E X.

B.

Beatrix,

C.

 people,

D.

frequent,

F.

I N D E X.

G.

H.

I.

Jews

K.

L.

Molina,

N.

O.

PADILLA,

N D E X.

P.

I N D E X.

R.

S.

Sesenas,

I N D E X.

T.

Tehya,

I N D E X.

X.

Y.

CPSIA information can be obtained
at www.ICGtesting.com
Printed in the USA
BVHW081003250619
551913BV00013B/444/P